For All The Jural A

FOR ALL THE JURAL ASSEMBLIES
by
"Anna von Reitz"

Anna Maria Riezinger
c/o Box 520994
Big Lake Alaska 99652

annavon@gmail.com
(907) 250-5087

Published by the Maine Republic Free State
Small Town, America

Contents

4   For All The Jural Assemblies

For All The Jural Assemblies

There seems to be a lot of confusion about the Jural Assemblies so I am writing this down for all the State Jural Assemblies at once. Although State Jural Assemblies are unique and dedicated to their individual State it is necessary for everyone to know basic definitions and oppositions and roles, so that everyone understands what they are doing and why.

Jural Assemblies are the organizational units of land and soil jurisdiction courts.

Jural Societies are the organizational units of sea and maritime jurisdiction courts.

Jural Assemblies "assemble". Jural Societies "associate".

Jural Assemblies create States and Counties.

Jural Societies create States of States and Counties Of _____.

As you can now fully appreciate from this brief description, both are necessary in order to properly conduct business on both land and sea.

States are geographically defined areas that are under the control of Public Laws established by the people who live within their borders. States are unincorporated land and soil jurisdiction entities run as unincorporated businesses. States have very simple names: Ohio, Rhode Island, Maine, Florida, Wisconsin, and so on.

In America, these States are joined together in a Union called a "Federation". The Federation is also unincorporated and is called "The United States of America". It was founded September 9, 1776.

All these organizational forms are created by living people, howbeit, people acting in two profoundly different capacities — as people, and as persons, incorporated entities.

People acting as people make up Jural Assemblies.

People acting as "persons" make up Jural Societies.

People acting in their unincorporated capacity as people who are members of a Jural Assembly decide the physical boundaries of their States, adopt the Public Laws within their States, and enforce the Public Law via their Jural Assemblies, their land and soil jurisdiction courts, and the officers of those courts.

Jural Assemblies organize the land and soil jurisdiction courts owed to the people of each State.

Jural Assembly organizers are responsible for making sure that candidate members are eligible to serve.

In most States, candidates must be at least 21, must have permanent homes declared within the geographic boundaries of their State, must be landowners (even if the land owned is only their reclaimed Good Name and bodily Estate), and at least until new elections are held within the Assembly to change the 1860 Conventions, the initial State Jural Assembly must be convened by white males meeting all other qualifications. This is because we are reopening courts that have been substantially (though not entirely) vacated since the Civil War.

People of Color and Women may be welcomed by all Jural Assemblies, but an "Update Election" must occur to open membership to all adult members of the community— with this one exception, that women may serve as proxies for their husbands upon the husband's grant of his agency to his wife. This basically means that she may act for her husband with his written consent in all matters stipulated as part of his grant of authority.

It is important to note that all people are part of the land and soil jurisdiction of their country, while "persons" are part of the sea and maritime jurisdiction.

As a result, land and soil jurisdiction courts

organized by Jural Assemblies are courts for the people.

Sea and maritime jurisdiction courts organized by Jural Societies are courts for unincorporated (trade) and incorporated (commercial) businesses — not people.

Please also note that no Jural Assemblies can be incorporated. They operate exclusively as unincorporated businesses and all their Officers and their members are operating in unincorporated capacity, too.

So, when you embark upon the adventure of creating a Jural Assembly you must (1) choose and declare that you are acting in your capacity as one of the "people" of this country, (2) you must record your choice with a land recording office formally re-conveying your Trade Name to the land and soil of your State, (3) you must accept the rights, responsibilities, and duties of a State Citizen when you act as a Juror or in any other Public Office of the Jural Assembly, (4) you must meet the basic requirements and thereby establish "standing" to act in the capacity of one of the People of your State.

Please note that land and soil are inextricably connected. Soil is defined as the first six inches — the very top layer — of the land, while land is all the underlying strata.

I am often asked — why can't People of Color and Women organize the initial Jural Assembly?

They can, they just can't make up part of the Quorum for a Jural Assembly until at least a minimum Jury Pool of originally qualified electors has been organized and has conducted an Update Election allowing membership to them. Again, this isn't anything arbitrary or racist or sexist. It is simply the fact that we are restoring a court system that hasn't been updated since 1860, and at that time, neither People of Color nor Women were allowed as part of the Quorum. That's why an "Update" Election is needed.

I am also often asked — why is it necessary to formally declare the capacity in which you are acting and also explicitly re-convey and claim your Trade Name? The short answer is that (1) you could get into trouble with federal Territorial authorities (what I call "Federales") if you don't, and (2) your Trade Name has already been shanghaied into the foreign jurisdiction of the sea, so, it requires official recorded (never registered) action on your part to "return" to the land and soil jurisdiction, which is a fundamental requirement for you to form a Jural Assembly (otherwise, all you could form would be a Jural Society).

Once everyone has done their paperwork and established their bona fides as people born on the land and soil of one of the American States or to parents or a parent born on the land and soil of one of the American States so as to be an Inheritor (this can go back three generations for those born in the unenrolled Western States*)

— you are ready to begin.

A Jural Assembly has Offices. All of these Offices are held in behalf of unincorporated business entities and are unincorporated Offices. Those Offices include the local Town and County Sheriffs entrusted with enforcement of the Public Law, the land jurisdiction State Judges (properly called "Justices") and the soil jurisdiction County Court Justices known as "Justices of the Peace". It also includes Court Clerks, Recorders, Bondsmen, Deputies, Public Notaries and Coroners.

All of these Offices are elected by members of the Jural Assembly who are the qualified Jurors making up the Jury Pool from which all Trial and Grand Juries are drawn by lot.

The land jurisdiction State Courts doing business simply as, for example, The Ohio State Court, enforce the Public and Organic Laws of Ohio including the provisions of The Constitution for the united States of America. The local County Courts also enforce these same laws, although there may be particular — even peculiar — local laws pertaining to soil and water and security issues of their soil jurisdiction.

All land and soil jurisdiction courts operate under the provisions of American Common Law. We do not practice Equity Law which is a hybrid of English Common Law and Admiralty Law.

The Land Jurisdiction County Sheriff is the highest ranking law enforcement officer in each County. All sea jurisdiction LEO's and corporate security personnel (Pinkertons) and subcontractors (Agency Personnel) report to your elected Land Jurisdiction County Sheriff — not the other way around.

Our Jural Assembly elections to fill the Offices of the Court are conducted as standard Public Elections, though all Electors must meet the same eligibility requirements as the members of the Jural Assembly. That is, you can't cross over and vote in the Private Corporate Elections of the Jural Societies, and they can't come over and vote in your Public Elections of the Jural Assemblies.

The two jurisdictions are mutually self-exclusive, as one cannot be on the land and on the sea at the same time.

Once your Jural Assembly Jury Pools are filled and your Officers have been elected, your Court is open for business — for your members only. As these are people Courts they deal only and exclusively with people business—issues of private property and assets, marriages, probate, and estates of people, rights of people, and so on. They can hear "Mixed Jurisdiction" cases in which people and unincorporated businesses have issues with other unincorporated or incorporated businesses, and Jural Assemblies can act as Parties to cases.

For example, People of Colorado versus Simon P. Jenkins and Sons, or People of Lords County v. IBM.

These are, essentially, the equivalent of "class action cases" in the land jurisdiction courts of our States and Counties.

They don't hear any issues arising among incorporated (commercial) entities. That is the business of the Jural Societies and their courts.

It is important to understand from the outset that these two court systems arising from the two different kinds of Jural Organizations under discussion (there are others) are completely separate hierarchies. Many people have grown up with the assumption that their State and their County are still functioning — and yes, they are, but just by the skin of their teeth.

The organizations that were at one point operating the land and soil Jural Assemblies have been largely displaced in many areas by private corporate courts operated by Jural Societies, instead. That is largely the result of the Great Fraud perpetuated by FDR and by the desire of many persons (as opposed to people) to share in federal racketeering kickbacks such as "Federal Block Grants".

Many auspices of our State and County and Local Government have been taken over via a surreptitious, secretive, and fraudulent undisclosed process of unlawful conversion, which takes place when a State or County organization is "converted" to operate as an incorporated "State of State" franchise of any foreign Territorial or Municipal Commercial Corporation.

No Jural Assembly, no actual State, no actual State Court, no actual County, and no actual County Court can be incorporated. Upon being incorporated, people become "persons" and the law of the land is converted to the law of the sea and the courts are operated by Jural Societies under international law instead of being operated by Jural Assemblies under National and local law.

If you think about it a moment you will see how the process of "incorporating" everything has been used to promote a de facto take over of our government and has led to the rampant criminality with which we now contend. You can also see how important it is for each one of us to get off our duffs and do the work.

Our unincorporated courts still stand over theirs and our people still stand over their persons —- but we must do this work of self-governance or we will have no country and no justice left. We must awaken our sleeping friends, families, and neighbors and ring the alarm. We must organize our Jural Assemblies and operate our States and Counties and re-enter all the Offices that have been secretively vacated.

Millions of us remain to be awakened and much work remains to be done, but there are now Jural Assemblies operating in every State of the Union. Find yours at:

www.national-assembly.net.

For All The Jural Assemblies - 2

Law And Religion

As I anticipated my release of "For All The Jural Assemblies" has stimulated quite a bit of discussion as more people are grasping the nature, function, and vital importance of our Jural Assemblies. As I also anticipated, this initial understanding is creating the need for more discussion of associated topics.

So here is Round Two: Our land and soil jurisdiction government is secular not religious, per se, for a reason. Our Founders were familiar with the evils of Theocracies and the way that such belief systems try to thwart the greater and more Universal Principle of Free Will, so they very decidedly and purposefully cast the issues of religious belief out of the American Government.

There is separation of Church and State to allow the peace and provide for just treatment of all those living under this system.

The basis of the American Common Law is the Ten Commandments which are "common" to all three major land based religions in the West– Judaism, Christianity, and Islam.

This common ethical basis provides the heart

of the Common Law– an ethical matrix that is "common" to and/or acceptable to adherents of all these major religions and most thinking people world wide.

In the vast main, people agree that one should not lie, cheat, steal, murder, and so on. The only significant exception to this is the religion of Satanism which is peculiar to the international jurisdiction of the sea and the realm of Commerce which pre-dates all the major western religions and includes premises that are very foreign to us.

Because of the separation of Church and State in this country, and because of the common law doctrine, none of our land jurisdiction Offices invoke God and they do not require Oaths of Office.

This will come as a big surprise to many people, but is obvious enough upon reflection.

The God of Israel is not the God of Judah and the God of Judah is not the God of Islam and the God of Islam is not the God of Christianity and the God of the Sea is not the God of any of the others, so our Forefathers who were familiar with this conundrum and were generally disposed to taking the Bible seriously did away with Oath-taking for Public Offices.

All those "swearing in" ceremonies we are familiar with and the phrase "so help me God" come from the sea jurisdiction courts, not the land and soil jurisdiction courts.

Oath-taking is a pagan custom and the "God" being appealed to is not necessarily "the" God most people assume it to be!

Because law comes from religion but is not in itself "a" religion there are many strange cross-overs, but generally speaking, the Law of the Land derives from the worship of Yahavah and the Law of the Sea derives from the worship of Baal (Satan) and the Law of the Air derives from the worship of Osiris.

Jural Assemblies as previously explained are constituted by people living on the land and soil of a country and whether Judaism, Islam, or Christianity is invoked, the same ethical standard of the Ten Commandments applies to everyone in Georgia as to everyone in Maine.

Jural Societies, on the other hand, are constituted by people acting as "Persons" existing in the realm of legal fictions — such as the mythical "State of Georgia" –and they uniformly apply the international Law of the Sea which is based on Baal worship and commercial codes descended from the Code of Hammurabi. This form of law is thoroughly pagan and predates all the major western religions by millennia.

By comparison the Law of the Sea functions by adages called "Maxims of Law" instead of by any simple and commonly accepted ethical precepts. The Maxims attempt to establish practical standards of "truth in commerce" and these paradoxically result from the worship of Satan, the Father of All Lies.

The theory behind the Law of the Sea is that we only know the truth by its opposite.

As a result of the foregoing, you now know why the Common Law is called "Common" and are further able to identify and distinguish between the Law of the Land and the Law of the Sea and between the Jural Assemblies and Jural Societies.

You also now know why land and soil jurisdiction Justices are elected and "confirmed" in Office but never "sworn" in, and why there is no mention of any "God" such as "So help me, God" in any land and soil jurisdiction court process.

As we restore our lawful –as opposed to "legal" courts and begin to function as Counselors in Law (Bar Members can function as "Counselors at Law") there is much to learn and remember.

We are vastly helped in this by the logic, simplicity and general familiarity of the Common Law, but in this process, Jural Assemblies must honor the Separation of Church and State, so as to further and additionally honor the Universal Principle of Free Will and Belief.

American Government is first and foremost designed to honor the inviolable rights of individual living people which include the freedom to choose what you believe in or don't believe in.

Those who wish to function in the capacity of living people and who accept the ethical foundation of the Ten Commandments as their Law are welcome to form their Jural Assemblies and Courts.

Those who wish to function in the capacity of legal fiction "Persons" and live under the restrictions of Commercial Code and pagan Maxims of Law are similarly welcome to form their Jural Societies and Courts.

And anyone who wishes to cross back and forth and make use of both court systems must be aware of what they are doing.

When FDR "flipped" everything upside down by presuming that everyone was choosing to act in the capacity of "Persons" instead of as "People" he set up a vast and unjustifiable Unlawful Conversion of our society and our system of justice.

The "Holy Cause" he mentioned in his First Inaugural Address was obviously an attempted "conversion" of a Christian country into a Baal-worshiping corporation accompanied by a non-consensual and fraudulent conversion of our assets as "presumed" chattel backing the debts of that corporation.

This Hideous Nonsense is now being addressed both nationally and internationally and the issues raised are being addressed openly.

Are you a Satan-worshiping pagan who believes in such practices as infanticide, or are you a Christian, Muslim, or adherent of Judaism?

If you are a Satan-worshiper you can just stay where FDR placed you and continue to act as a "Person" obligated to function under the international Law of the Sea.

Everyone else needs to correct the falsified public records, explicitly remove their Trade Names back to permanent domicile on the land and soil States and get their Jural Assemblies set up.

www.national-assembly.net
or email
contactmanager1@yahoo.com.

For All The Jural Assemblies - 3

This is <u>NOT</u> "opinion"

What I am pointing out to you and everyone else is not a topic for "argument". It isn't my "opinion". It is the way the world's court system has been organized for centuries and just because 99% of Americans are too ignorant to know that and have been deliberately kept too dumbed-down to learn it, does not make it any less true and factual.

Now, you have a choice. You can be a landsman and reclaim your country and your "Natural and Unalienable" rights, and you can enforce the Constitution you are owed, and you can enjoy your freedom and you can join your Jural Assembly and you can operate your State, or you can sit on your rump and blow your mouth and spin — and the British King will be happy to take all your assets and dump them into a Commonwealth Trust (that he controls and benefits from) and designate you as a "pauper" and a dependent of his government—-your choice.

If you want Choice A, help establish, staff, and organize a Jural Assembly.

If you want Choice B, help establish, staff, and organize a Jural Society.

Please note that this is not only "American Corruption" — this same situation applies worldwide. The only exceptions are Iran, North Korea, the Holy See, and a handful of Pacific Island Kingdoms.

And now for another repeat of a Vital History Lesson for All Americans and All Jural Assemblies:

1. The United States (unincorporated) was formed on July 1, 1776, as a result of the Unanimous Declaration of Independence. The members of this Union were all Colonies and they also operated as "the United Colonies of America". This is not to be confused with Benjamin Franklin's private business (also unincorporated) doing business as "the" United States.

2. The United States of America (unincorporated) was formed on September 9, 1776, by a declaration of the Continental (that's land jurisdiction) Congress.

This Holding Company is a Federation of unincorporated geographically defined States: Ohio, Pennsylvania, Maine, etc.

3. The States of America (unincorporated) was formed March 1, 1781, by Agreement of the States ratified as The Articles of Confederation. This was a Confederacy of States of States created to conduct commercial business in behalf of the Federation States. The members of

this original Confederacy went by names like this: The State of Georgia, The State of Virginia, The State of Maine….

4. The original Confederation adopted and became the recipients of the service contract known as "The Constitution for the united States of America" in 1787. If you can read and know anything at all about English grammar you can observe from this that the word "united" is used here as an adjective to describe "States of America" and references their "union" created under The Articles of Confederation. This Confederacy of "States of States" is the actual Party to the 1787 Constitution.

5. In 1860-61, the Southern States of States in the original Confederacy left the organization doing business as the "States of America" — "seceded from it" — and formed a new and separate confederacy called "The Confederate States of America".

6. The entire Civil War was thus a commercial mercenary conflict between the Northern States of States operating under the States of America Confederacy and the Southern States of States operating under The Confederate States of America.

7. After the end of hostilities the British Monarch saw his chance to pull a fast one, by claiming that the Federal States of States were under "Reconstruction" and then, very quietly, creat-

ing an incorporated Scottish commercial corporation merely calling itself "The United States of America" [Incorporated] and substituting franchises of this corporation [formed in Scotland in 1868 — we have the paperwork and proof] for the original Federal States of States. Thus, "The State of Florida" owned and operated by Florida for the benefit of Floridians, was moth-balled, and a Territorial franchise corporation calling itself by the deceptively similar name "the State of Florida" owned and operated by the Scottish Government for the benefit of the British Monarch and United Kingdom, took its place —- and generations of Americans have been kept none the wiser.

Well, now you are all "the Wiser".

You must take control of your own government. You must accept the responsibilities that go with the rights of self-government, or your assets will be plundered and pillaged to enrich the British Monarch and the Papacy, you will permanently be enslaved as a population, and you will have no claim left to the land and soil of your own country.

When I say it is time to "Wake up!" and form your Jural Assemblies, it isn't just my opinion. A National Trust like any other property trust can only endure for three (3) generations before being renewed, otherwise, it is liquidated and there is no longer any interest preserved for the heirs.

It has been three generations since these con artists began their scheme.

My husband and I climbed out from under their rock in 1998. In 2015 we re-issued our Sovereign Letters Patent and this affords you the opportunity to extend your National Trust for another three generations— IF you all get busy and operate your States and form your Jural Assemblies and act in the capacity of living heirs — as people, not persons.

I don't know what I can say or do to make this any clearer for all of you. You are in grave danger of being defrauded out of your entire inheritance — your land and soil, your businesses and homes, your labor, your bodies, and your Good Name. These criminals have conspired to steal it all right from under your noses, just as Thomas Jefferson said they would, if you were not "vigilant".

Well, my husband and I and many others have been "vigilant" and that is why you all continue to have a reprieve to gain knowledge and not be destroyed, but it is time for you to take action. It is completely safe and proper, peaceful and unarguable for you to reclaim your Good Name and remove it to its original domicile on the land and soil of your home State. Do so.

Remember that all the Delegated Powers that were ever exercised by the Confederation States of States were delegated to them by the States acting through their Federation, The United States of America [Unincorporated]— not the other way around.

You have to have a Florida before you can create "The State of Florida", much less "the State of Florida" or "the STATE OF FLORIDA".

Thus, when the original Federal States of States were inoperable after the Civil War, those Delegated Powers returned by Operation of Law to the Issuers of those "powers" — to the actual States and their Federation of States, owned and operated by the living people. Not the King of England.

There is a great deal more history to all of this, but it all comes down to understanding who and what you are. Are you one of the living people of this country, a lawful inheritor? Or are you a mere "person" acting as surety for a bankrupt commercial corporation in "equitable exchange" for benefits doled out by bankruptcy trustees?

If you are one of the people, it is high time to reclaim your Good Name, correct the falsified records being held against you, and join your State Jural Assembly.

Please note that you are guaranteed the right to peaceably "assemble" — but not guaranteed the right to "associate". This is because people are sovereign and unincorporated entities, while "persons" are (in this case, foreign) corporate franchises owing obedience to the parent corporations that own them.

We have bought you time and kept your lawful claims alive, but you MUST wake up now and get moving in your own behalf and for the sake of your country and your children.

A foul white-collar fraud scheme promoted first by the Government of Scotland and next by officers of the Roman Catholic Church has very nearly succeeded in stealing your National Trust and reducing you all to chattel backing the debts of bankrupt commercial corporations "forever".

Get on your feet. Understand what has happened and what must be done to answer it. Take back your Good Name and Estate, by formally re-conveying them to the land and soil of your home State. The paperwork to do this is on my website: www.annavonreitz.com, Article 928.

Then go to www.national-assembly.net or email contentmanager1@yahoo.com

Some of you have been trying to form Jural Societies in the mistaken idea that you could re-construct the Federal States of States by doing so, but the horse has to go in front of the cart— or you will get nowhere and waste a lot of time and energy in the process.

For All The Jural Assemblies - 4

Juror Qualifications and Membership

I get a lots of pleas for help and instructions for the Jural Assemblies. So, first things first. You have to qualify potential Jurors. Not just everyone can walk in off the street and function as a Juror. A Juror is a temporary State Citizen for the duration of their Jury Duty, and as such, must qualify as an Elector of that State as well as a State National under our established system of government.

It may at first sound daunting, but the process is only a reflection of the seriousness of the duty being performed. You wouldn't want to entrust your life to a surgeon with no first aid training, and in the same way, you do not want to entrust your fate to unqualified Jurors.

So– yes, the first business to be addressed is the declared political status of the candidate. That begins with establishing whether or not they were born in this country or born to a parent or parents born in this country (This provision goes back three generations as a result of the National Trust.)

The List:

*Proof of American Nationality.

*Proof of Identity

*Act of Expatriation from Territorial or Municipal Citizenship

*Recorded Acknowledgement, Acceptance and Re-Conveyance of Trade Name

*Recorded Declaration of Permanent Domicile of the Trade Name on the Land and Soil of the State

*Recorded Certificate of Assumed Names/ NAMES claiming ownership and declaring permanent domicile of all Names/NAMES used by or associated with the Juror

*Copy of Form 56 (Social Security Number redacted) and mailing receipts demonstrating that the Municipal PERSON ACCOUNTS have been returned to and made the responsibility of the United States Secretary of the Treasury.

Step One: Require Birth Certificates or public documents that adequately establish the location where each candidate Juror was born, or in the case of those people claiming their nationality via parents/grandparents, similar documentation establishing the parents/grandparents place of birth and political status as American State Nationals.

Step Two: Require the direct corroboration of at least two (2) people who have reasonable first hand knowledge allowing them to attest that the candidate Juror is the man or woman whose birth and parentage is established by the records being presented in Step One. This can be done via the direct testimony of the Witnesses or via their written testimony under penalty of perjury. The Witnesses must sign and give their contact information in either case. Typically, Witnesses will be a family member or old family friends who have known the family and the potential Juror a long time.

Step Three: Once you have established that you have an eligible Juror who qualifies as a birthright American, the candidate must confirm his agreement to formally expatriate from British Territorial Citizenship and also from any Municipal United States Citizenship conferred upon him or her, and sign a Witnessed Act of Expatriation formally claiming their Nationality from their State of Origin or to their Inherited State of Origin (in the case of those claiming via parents and grandparents). This will be one of the States in existence prior to 1860 and may or may not be the same State as the State where the Jural Assembly is taking place—or as we shall see, even different from the "State" where they were actually born.

Step Four: Candidates for the First Initiating Jural Assembly must be: (1) at least 21 years of age, (2) white, (3) males (4) landowners in the State. This is because we are restoring and updating from 1860, a time long prior to the 18-year-old age of majority and votes for women and colored people. At the initial meeting, it is highly recommended that those initiating members open up the Jural Assembly membership to include women and colored people as Electors and Jurors. It is also recommended that they retain the Age of Majority at 21 and the landowner requirements, as they are in place to guarantee a membership having familiarity with life beyond High School and also, as landowners, having a firm attachment to the State and reason to work for its overall benefit.

Step Five: Although an informed Act of Expatriation witnessed by two or more people should be sufficient evidence of will and intent in the matter of political status, it is not in itself sufficient to establish ownership of our Good Names (also known as Trade Names and Given Names) and Estates which must be unencumbered and untangled from the morass of false presumptions, conferred political statuses, and false claims that have been amassed against our true identities.

Therefore it is prudent and wise for each candidate Juror to formally seize upon, acknowledge, accept, and re-convey their Trade Name (Upper and Lower Case: John Paul Jones, for example) and to declare and record its permanent domicile on the land and soil of their home or birth State.

This is a process akin to re-flagging a ship under new ownership and provides evidence of transfer of ownership interest and obligations of law to an actual State of the Union, instead of a Territorial State of State of Municipal STATE OF STATE. Instructions for this are posted at www.annavonreitz.com, Article 928.

The reasons for taking this step are: (1) to secure the ownership interest in one's own Name, and therefore, create the basis for claiming back one's own ESTATE and control over one's own affairs; (2) to prevent any interference from or claims by Federal Agents allowing them to address us or our Jural Assemblies under false pretenses; (3) to assure that the actions of our Jural Assemblies are unassailable.

If we have a twelve man jury and even one of them can still be mis-characterized as a British Territorial or Municipal "Citizen" the deliberations and validity of the jury as a whole can be questioned, as our States do not allow Dual Citizenship. Please underline that fact.

The Federales both Territorial and Municipal allow Dual Citizenship, but the American States do not.

Step Six: For the same reason as those cited above with respect to Trade Names, it is also highly recommended and desirable for candidate Jurors to seize upon and declare a permanent domicile for the Municipal NAMES that have been conferred upon us using the Certificate of Assumed Name Form (Article 928 on my website) and including every possible variation of every name ever used by or associated with them including Married Names, Pen Names, Performer Names, etc. You should include any business names and as many styles and permutations and punctuations of your name as you can think of as well as the general claim for "all, any and sundry variations, combinations, abbreviations, punctuations, orderings, styles and representations of any name, Name, or NAME associated with you, your Trade Name, or your business enterprises in any jurisdiction of law whatsoever."

Step Seven: It is advisable that a copy of the Territorial/Municipal Birth Certificate be returned and canceled via proper signature "without recourse" and dated and returned to the US Secretary of the Treasury and the US Secretary of State along with a Form 56 designating one and/or both as Fiduciary for the PERSON. Again, this covers the bases regarding any presumed Dual Citizenship and denies any conflict of interest on the part of potential Jurors. It also makes the Fiduciaries responsible for Good Faith administration of these ACCOUNTS and the bookkeeping and payments related to them— relieving the rest of us of any such duty or obligation.

False "citizenships" have been arbitrarily "conferred" on you based on a false presumption that you or have ever been "stateless", seeking to obligate you and seize upon your assets as collateral backing the debts of the perpetrators of this scheme, so it is important for your own sakes as well as the proper and unquestionable functioning of the Jural Assembly for you to return these false "gifts" whence they came. This further proves up and gives evidence of your intent to be free of any claim of foreign "personhood" and your equal determination to reclaim your status as one of the "people" of this country.

Upon the completion of these steps, the candidate Juror may be "seated" as a Qualified Juror and member of a specific County Jural Assembly and State Jural Assembly.

Please Note:

1. Whereas colored people and women cannot act as Jurors or Electors until an Initial Jural Assembly with a Quorum of 15 Members has been called and has voted to update the rules to allow their participation, they can and should assist in the entire process of recruiting and establishing their State Jural Assembly in anticipation of full participation being open to them immediately after the Initial Jural Assembly meets. We need every loyal living American helping and assisting this process as we go forward.

2. The Western States that did not join the Union until after the Civil War are in an odd status, as they have been guaranteed all the rights and interests of the older States, but have not been formally enrolled as States. This is another Swindle that has been attempted by the perpetrators in Washington, DC, and unfortunately, it cannot be corrected until a Continental Congress addresses the situation and approves their formal enrollment. This situation means that people born in these Western States are born as de facto Territorial Citizens and must take recourse to establish their Nationality via their parents and grandparents.

For example, my husband was born in Washington State, which is a land trust "State". His Father and Grandfather were also born in Western States, but because the National Trust Guarantee lasts for three generations, each one preserves the option of exercising their "reversionary trust interest"— so, although James Clinton Belcher was born in Washington State, and his Father and Grandfather were similarly afflicted by the above-described situation, he can claim all the way back to his Great-Grandfathers and Mothers, who were Virginians and Pennsylvanians.

This is where the saying "Grandfathered in" comes from, though it is often applied to things other than the National Trust.

In practical terms, then, some Jural Assemblies in the Western States will have a bit harder time documenting their membership as the candidates will, unless they were born in one of the pre-1860 States, need to track back in the records to establish an ancestor of proven American State Nationality.

3. American State Nationals are not obligated to serve as Jural Assembly Members; Jural Assembly Members are volunteering to preserve their land jurisdiction States and their Court Systems—without which there is no country and no private ownership of anything. Please note — a National has no obligation to the Government, whereas a Citizen has an obligation to his or her State so long as they are serving in a Public Office, such as Juror. Their obligation may be relatively temporary (as when actually serving as a Juror) or for a Term in Office, like a Justice of the Peace or a Coroner.

4. Land Ownership is a tricky qualification of Jurors. In the past, in a pinch, the "land and soil" that a man owns can be defined as his body: "Dust thou art and to dust returneth." but I would argue and it is wise that Jural Assembly Members should be attached to their State via the establishment of permanent homes and property interests in that State. The initial qualification for immigrants to become State Nationals requires them to live in a State for at least "one year and a day" with no felony arrests and no claims for Public Assistance and to establish a permanent home or dwelling within the borders

of the State. I believe that the qualifications for Jural Assembly Members should meet that criterion also.

5. People who are landowners in one or more States can theoretically participate in the different State Jural Assemblies sequentially and if they meet the other qualifications and if at least one year has passed between such incidents of participation per the one year requirement discussed above, —otherwise, it could run afoul of the "No Dual Citizenship" provisions of all the States.

For example, say that I own a home in Wisconsin and a winter vacation home in Texas for a number of years. If I lived in Wisconsin for fifty years and participated in that Jural Assembly, I could move to my retirement home in Texas and qualify as a member of the Texas Jural Assembly after actually living at my Texas home for a year and a day— and not have to go through all the rest of the qualification process again. Jural Assembly membership once established is therefore somewhat transferrable, but at no time can one belong to two State Jural Assemblies at the same time as that would violate the "No Dual Citizenship" provisions of the land and soil jurisdiction States.

6. Nationality can be established in a State different than the State of one's Jural Assembly and this is more common than not with today's mobile population. In most of the Western States

(California, Oregon, and Texas excepted) it is a given that the Jural Assembly members will have established their Nationality claims elsewhere. For example, a man born in Maine may migrate to California and join the California Jural Assembly and his American State Nationality requirement is still met by being born in Maine. There is no requirement that he be born in California to serve on the California Jural Assembly, so long as he is born in or otherwise lawfully able to claim his nationality from one of the actual States of the Federation Union.

7. The Federal States of States, like The State of Pennsylvania that were members of the original Confederation of States doing business as the States of America, were moth-balled and substituted "for" during the Reconstruction Era. They still exist as State Land Trusts which we are the lawful inheritors of.

For example, the Ohio State is a trust established to hold the assets and contracts owed to The State of Ohio, which has been moth-balled since 1868, and both the Trust and everything in it is owed to Ohio and the Ohioans — so long as they claim it, which they do by exercising their capacity to act as one of the People of Ohio and forming their State Jural Assemblies.

I hope that the importance and urgency of claiming your rightful inheritance including these State Land Trusts, are now fully dawning on all of those reading this and that you will not hesitate or lack motivation to complete the Juror Qualifications and join your State Jural Assembly.

8. Finally, I recommend that every State Jural Assembly adopt a simple explicit Mission Statement and Membership Agreement so that there can be no doubt about what the Jural Assembly is, who the members are, what capacity everyone is acting in, and the intentions and purposes of the group.

This is needed for those in the group, those joining the group, and those Federales snooping around the edges "investigating" the group for any sign of rebellion or insurrection. I will provide a basic template in a separate article.

My website www.annavonreitz.com (Article 928) has examples of the paperwork to reclaim and domicile your Good Name and ESTATE interests, and www.natonal-assembly.net can put you in contact with your State organization. For specific help, you may also email: contentmanager1@yahoo.com.

For All The Jural Assemblies - 5

Mission Statement and Membership Agreement

The Mission Statement for any organization worth its salt should be short and sweet and exact and as explicit as humanly possible, so as to conclusively answer the questions— "What are we doing and why?" In the case of the State Jural Assemblies the answer to these questions is exactly the same all across the board—- for example:

Mission Statement for the Wisconsin Jural Assembly

Our Wisconsin Jural Assembly is dedicated to the restoration of a complete and fully operational land and soil jurisdiction State and County court system serving the people of Wisconsin, the preservation of the National Trust, the enforcement of the Public Law, the upholding of the Federal Constitution owed to our State and People, the re-population of our land and soil jurisdiction, the filling of vacated Public Offices, and the reclamation of our material and intellectual public and private assets.

To these ends, we, the living people of Wisconsin, have called the eligible Wisconsin Nationals and Electors to assemble and to serve as Jurors and Officers, and we have established the process and procedure to qualify Jurors and others competent to hold State Citizenship and Public Office. We do this peacefully and without rancor in the exercise of our unincorporated powers and capacities.

The above Mission Statement pretty much nails down who is doing what and in what capacity and why. That's all a Mission Statement needs.

Now for the Membership Agreement portion — again, using Wisconsin as an example:

Wisconsin Jural Assembly Membership Agreement

In acknowledging and accepting the duties of a Wisconsin Jural Assembly Member, I act without any deceit or profit motive or obligation. I affirm that I am one of the people of Wisconsin and that I am acting exclusively in my natural and unincorporated capacity. I affirm that I have expatriated from any presumed citizenship obligation owed to the Territorial United States and/or to the Municipal United States and I make no claim of Dual Citizenship and hold no allegiance to any foreign power at all. I affirm by this testament that I am qualified and able and willing to act as a Wisconsin Citizen, as a Wisconsin Juror, and as a Wisconsin Elector and do so of my own free will and I also say that there is to my best knowledge and belief no circumstance or obligation barring me from occupying any vacated Wisconsin Public Office or preventing me from providing Good Faith Service in such Office if I am elected. In accepting the duties of a Wisconsin Jural Assembly Member I also accept the rights and responsibilities thereof. I understand that I may be called upon to serve as a member of a Grand Jury, or a Trial Jury, or to act as a Sheriff's Deputy, or to act as a Witness to Public or Private Records, and that I may be asked to serve in similar capacities with or without pay. I accept my duty to serve Wisconsin and my fellow Wisconsinites without reservation, coercion, or issue of conscience. I understand that I am, as a Wisconsin Citizen, responsible for upholding the Public and Organic Law of Wisconsin and that if I should be elected or appointed or otherwise entrusted with assets belonging to Wisconsin or any County thereof, I am obligated to act as a deputy and as a fiduciary under the Prudent Man Standard until relieved of such duty. As a member of the Wisconsin Jural Assembly, I shall faithfully promote and help secure Justice for all people, through the right use of Due Process and Jury Nullification. I shall at all times endeavor to keep the peace and to know and uphold the best standards and traditions of the American Common Law. So say I and witness my autograph and

thumbprint seal as I commit myself to serve as
a member of the Wisconsin Jural Assembly this
_____ day of _____ in the year _____
before these Witnesses:

by: _____ (Seal)
living at 1101 Bollingbrook Street in Racine,
Wisconsin.

Witnessed by:

_____

living at

_____.

Witnessed by:

_____

living at

_____.

\>>><<

    Ideally, the Witnesses will also be Jural As-
sembly Members and the records will be kept in
original triplicate, one copy to the new Juror,
one to the Juror's home County, one to be kept
by the State Jural Assembly.

It is advisable to design and secure the unique use of a distinctive Jural Assembly stamp and/ or Logo to be used as a Letterhead on these records.

Although there may be some additional or different issues each Jural Assembly may wish to address, the verbiage given here is precise and correct for the jurisdiction invoked: we do not, for example, use "affidavits" and we do not "swear" any oaths or make reference to "God" in the land and soil jurisdiction courts.

The confirmations of Public Offices are simple affirmations of duties and obligations undertaken due to the Separation of Church and State in the actual American government.

Though familiar to us, swearing oaths is a pagan practice of commercial courts, the phrase "so help me God" we grew up hearing from Perry Mason and on other court dramas, is also. It was not used in American Courts until the Unlawful Conversion of our Court System by FDR.

The actual land and soil jurisdiction courts operate on the principle of "Let your yes be yes and your no be no." Instead of affidavits, we use testamentary evidence and instead of swearing to anything under penalty of perjury, we use affirmations "to the best of our knowledge and belief from without the United States".

For All The Jural Assemblies - 6

Pointers and Questions

There are some issues being brought forward by various parties, some of whom are confused and others who just want me to address specific issues, so this is a nuts and bolts presentation of information that isn't coordinated around any specific theme beyond answering questions people have.

1. What is Mr. Trump's Republic about? The reforms they are making sound great and in line with what you are doing. Should we just wait and see what happens before we make all this effort to form Jural Assemblies?

Answer: Remember there are two (2) gangs, one Territorial and one Municipal, and neither one is supposed to be running this country.

It is the right, duty and responsibility of the actual people in each State to operate their Federation of States to run this country, and in order to do that, they must take up the work of forming their State Jural Assemblies. Forming and operating our State Jural Assemblies is the only way to fully restore the government we are supposed to have — i.e., finish the Reconstruction– and then determine where we want to go from there.

Mr. Trump is fully honoring his duty as Commander in Chief and protecting America and Americans. For that, he is to be lauded and loved. A great many other Presidents have grossly abused their position of trust and have allowed personal cowardice and/or self-interest to enter into their decision-making processes. I respect Donald Trump and so should everyone else. He does not act as a lobbyist for the Republican Party and he does not back down for the Democrat lobbyists, either. He charts a course that is best for America as a whole and keeps steady on.

We should all be grateful to and for Donald Trump— including the millions of rank-and-file Democrats who have listened to their party leadership and the so-called "mainstream media" instead of using their own eyes and noses.

Whatever Donald Trump's piccadillo roster may include, he is: (1) devoted to America; (2) an excellent businessman; (3) a generous heart. He has, without undue pressure on the Public Purse, vastly increased employment opportunities — especially for women, blacks, and Hispanics, expanded our economy, regained control of destructive trade agreements, and is working to secure our border — without which, we don't have a country anymore.

The gross self-interest and if I may say so, stupidity, of the Municipal Government leadership has led to unnecessary suffering that is entirely the fault of the members of the Congress and the bought-and-paid-for Press Corps, a social class of dishonest, arrogant pretenders who all pull their stories off the same wire services instead of doing anything resembling actual investigative journalism, yet want us to respect and trust their opinions as "law". They are parroting whatever comes in via the Associated Press (and who are they?) and Reuters (and who are they?) and that has been the degraded and deplorable condition of American Journalism for decades.

Mr. Trump is exactly right when he calls them "Fakes" — they are pretending to be journalists and not doing the job. They are in fact functioning as well-paid lobbyists and propagandists with no great respect for facts or law, and are the ones pushing former CIA Chief Hayden's vision of a "Post Truth Society" — i.e., a world run on the basis of lies, lies, and more lies.

A virtual war has been and is being fought in Hollywood, California, among those who espouse this criminal insanity and those who do not.

So — no, we can't afford to sit on our rumps at the stadium and watch the show and do nothing but "hope" that the Territorial Team wins. We do have to get motivated and set up our

State (and County) Jural Assemblies and do the work. Now.

2. Shouldn't all State Assembly Members cancel their Voter Registrations?

Yes, they have to. This goes back to the requirement that all the actual land and soil jurisdiction State governments have forbidding Dual Citizenship. You are either in or out, so far as the States are concerned. The Territorial and Municipal Governments both allow Dual Citizenship, but in establishing and operating the State Jural Assemblies we have to work for our State and conduct its business.

This goes back to the principle of "Checks and Balances" — you can't allow your employees to write their own job descriptions, set their own pay and benefits, and supervise all their own activities — which is precisely what has been going on in this country for far too long. The Territorial and Municipal Governments are both supposed to be dependent on the States to ride herd on their spending and activities. We are supposed to be holding them to their obligations under the terms of the Constitutions that apply to them.

In 1868, approximately nine (9) million Americans were "disenfranchised" as the original Federal States of States were moth-balled and the Territorial States of States were substituted. Virtually nobody understood what was actually going on, because of the deceitfully similar names employed: "The State of Maine" versus "the State of Maine", for example.

However and in fact, this change meant that people were forced to give up their "voting rights" as shareholders in one set of corporations and to either accept or forego "voting rights" in a new set of corporations. When people transferred their "voting rights" to the interlopers, they unwittingly entered a new jurisdiction— that of the British Territorial United States — and lost their birthright position on the land and soil jurisdiction of the States by unconsciously accepting Dual Citizenship.

They lost their ability to function as State Electors as a direct result and became British "subjects". This is precisely what the King wanted and what he achieved via fraud and unconscionable contracts and gross Breach of Trust. Millions of Americans were thus "converted" from their natural birthright political status and subjected to the whims of the British King, without their knowledge or consent—-simply by "doing their duty" and continuing to "vote" in what appeared to be normal public elections.

That was the First Great Fraud against the American States and People, carried out by our own paid military and federal municipal employees and our International Trustees — the British Monarch and the Pope, both of whom were, and are, completely culpable.

So yes, all State Assembly Members must cancel and expunge all Voter Registrations and cannot continue to vote in these foreign corporation elections without accepting Dual Citizenship and thereby making themselves ineligible to function as State Citizens.

You may think — but that's crazy! I won't be able to control who is in the White House or in the Territorial Congress! I will be giving up whatever little bit of influence I have on the direction this country is heading!

Remember that their system is all rigged and set up as two gangs— your vote determines very little in their matrix, and since the advent of hackable Diebold voting machines, your vote arguably determines nothing at all. Also, remember that whether the issue at hand is "Territorial" or "Municipal" both are employees of the States. Once you take up your position as the Employer, you actually have far more power than any mere "voter" in their system. It is as a State Citizen and Elector that you have the contractual ability to control them.

You will also be doing your part to restore the rightful American Government this country is owed. Operating as a State Citizen and/or State Elector allows you to finish the restoration — also known as "reconstruction"— of the Federal States of States, which are supposed to be owned and controlled and operated for the benefit of your State, not the UK and certainly not the Holy Roman Empire.

3. We are confused about which State or States we are supposed to be restoring? You talk about setting up the State Jural Assemblies and then talk about reconstructing the Federal States of States — ?

Ah. It's important to realize that the actual States have never been involved in any of the chaos and chicanery affecting the States of States.

We are so used to seeing "State of Missouri" and "State of Alabama" and so on, that we started thinking of these organizations as "the" States, but in fact, they are not.

The States are operated by the people living in the State.

The States of States are operated by employees of the people living in the States.

The States have been "missing in action" because the people have not known that it is their right and responsibility and duty to assemble their State Jural Assemblies. They've been "letting George do it" — literally, and for far too long.

Because the people are sovereign and unincorporated and running the actual State is their business, it has been nobody's right or responsibility to tell them that they have to assemble and conduct business—- except that the Heredi-tary Head of State operating The United States of America (the unincorporated version) can call upon them to assemble as the leader of their Federation of States.

So, that is what has happened.

You have all been summoned to assemble your State Jural Assemblies, to operate your States, elect your Officers, set up your land and soil jurisdiction courts, re-construct your Fed-eral States of State, exercise your position as an Employer, and reclaim your birthright.

Doing so is absolutely necessary at this time, because the National Trust endures for only three (3) generations and the tail end of those three (3) generations has come. We have taken the proper steps to re-issue our Sovereign Letters Patent to update and renew the National Trust, and now you all need to get off your duffs and pull together your State Jural Assemblies.

It is true that we need to "re-construct" the Federal States of States to act in behalf of the States, but only the People of the States can do any of this—the State Citizens of each State must act to restore the Federal State of State they are owed. Thus it becomes necessary for us to step forward, identify ourselves as one of the "People" instead of acting in the capacity of a foreign "Person" — and assemble the State first. Then we can reconstruct the Federal State of State.

You can't have any form of "State of Florida" without a Florida, can you?

The very existence of a "State of Florida" depends on the existence of "Florida" and the existence of "Florida" depends on the existence of the "People" of Florida —- which means the State Citizens making up the State Jural Assembly.

So, it's showtime, folks.

Will the actual People please stand up?

4. Can you please explain how all this sleight of hand works? The substitution of one thing for another?

There are two classic and fundamental such sleights of hand that have led to all the others.

The First Great Fraud, as I have described elsewhere, came just after Civil War when a Scottish Commercial Corporation secretively infringed upon the name of our unincorporated Federation of States and called itself "The United States of America" [Incorporated].

This then was further exacerbated by the same scoundrels deceitfully naming corporate franchises of their new corporation after our Federal States of States. In this scam "The State of Virginia" (Federal) was replaced by "the State of Virginia" (Territorial). And except for some attorneys, Territorial Congress members, and guilty Generals, the populace was kept in the dark and fed horse hunks.

The result was that instead of the States being properly represented and benefiting from their own Federal States of States, all the Federal States of States were moth-balled as assets belonging to the land jurisdiction States, and the Territorial States of States were set up to operate for the benefit of the British Monarch and the UK.

We were diddled, left in the dark, and over time, those who knew the whole story were picked off, forced to flee under threat of death (like my husband's family), or died of natural causes —- until now, three generations later, people are in a daze without any idea of what went on here, much less how to fix it and address the problem.

So I am telling you right here and now — the way to address it is to reclaim your birthright trust interest, operate in your unincorporated capacity as a State Citizen, and join and operate your State Jural Assembly. Your State organization — your State Jural Assembly — can then reconstruct your Federal State of State to your heart's delight and operate it, too— for your benefit and the benefit of your State, instead of for the benefit of the UK or the Holy Roman Empire—both of which merely have a service contract that they have abused beyond any rational standard.

The Second Great Fraud happened in 1933 under the aegis of the great King Rat himself, FDR.

This was also a sleight of hand substitution fraud favoring England and the "Holy Roman Empire"/ Office of the Roman Pontiff / Romanus Pontifex Trust.

In the First Great Fraud they substituted "The United States of America" Incorporated for "The United States of America" —Unincorporated, and the Federal States of States, for example, "The State of Georgia" and "The State of Maine" for Territorial States of States operating under very similar names: "the State of Georgia" and "the State of Maine" —- only the beneficiaries had changed — from the American States and People to the British Monarch and the UK.

In the Second Great Fraud under FDR, they substituted all our "People" for their "Persons".

It is much the same schtick, only instead of undermining our Federation of States via identity theft and usurping upon our Federal States of States by substituting their own Territorial States of States — under FDR, they stole your identity, too.

Here is how they did it, and it is a very similar fraud:

Under the Constitutions and Treaties associated with them, the British Monarch is named as our Trustee "on the High Seas and Inland Waterways". Thus it is, that when we venture out on "the High Seas" and "Inland Waterways" we have unknowingly been wards of the King. He is obligated to protect us and see to our welfare. The Government of Westminster is similarly obligated to aid and protect us.

So, to get around this and have an excuse to plunder and pillage us, they pretended that we "set sail" and were "lost at sea". That provided the excuse to set up Cestui Que Vie ESTATE trusts in Puerto Rico named after each and every one of us.

The British Monarch and the Pope acting as Pontiff then eagerly charged off all the "services" they were providing via the Territorial United States corporations and the Municipal United States corporations against these phony Territorial Trusts ("John Philip Miller" a Territorial Foreign Situs Trust) and equally phony Municipal ESTATES ("JOHN PHILIP MILLER") and phony Municipal PUBLIC UTILITIES ("JOHN P. MILLER") and phony Municipal CHARITABLE TRUSTS (JOHN MILLER).

They then also unleashed the members of the Bar Associations on us (Territorial Government) to act as Licensed Privateers, and unleashed the "Internal Revenue Service" to act as Bill Collectors. Our Public Courts were converted to run as private corporate bill collection agencies, the Middlemen in this scheme — our

Employees — were mistaken for the actual Employers.

In this secretive way, our country and its lawful government were completely usurped by banal traitors and our States were purportedly "de-populated" and we ourselves were falsely subjected to foreign powers and treated as slaves in our own country.

The Lynch Pin in this scam was our innocent unincorporated Trade Name given to us by our parents. This Trade Name, also known as a Given Name, allows us to conduct both local in-state and international trade within the land and soil jurisdiction of our country.

Remember that America is a little bit odd, in that every State is a Nation. This results in a situation where "interstate" trade is the same as "international" trade.

Also remember the definition of "trade" involves business between unincorporated businesses and unincorporated businesses and corporations, while "commerce" involves business between two incorporated entities.

Trade: John Philip Miller operating in unincorporated natural capacity buys widgets from 3M Corporation and a glass of lemonade from Sally Lou Jenkins.

Commerce: John Philip Miller (Inc.) operating in the capacity of a franchise corporation of

"The United State, Inc." buys widgets from 3M Corporation.

See the difference?

Only "commerce" is under any form of "federal" control.

Acting in his unincorporated capacity, John Philip Miller, is engaged in peaceful private international trade.

Acting in any incorporated capacity, John Philip Miller is engaged in public commerce, and is doing so as a franchisee of a parent corporation.

This is the kind of "enfranchisement" the rats were talking about vis-a-vis voting — to take in all your assets, commandeer them as chattel backing their filthy commercial corporations, and subject you to both the British Territorial Government and the Pope's Municipal Government.

Looking at the name, "John Philip Miller", it is impossible to tell which capacity the man is operating in, so FDR just arbitrarily "decided" for his own self-interest, to change the legal presumptions of the day, and falsely claim that all the people in America were voluntarily acting as franchises of his favorite bankrupted Roman Catholic non-profit corporation doing business as "the United States of America" Incorporated--which is just a later version of the original Scottish fraud and national identity theft scheme promoted by the Holy See and the Holy Roman Empire instead.

This allowed the Plotters to commandeer our assets, our Good Names, our private property, even our bodies— so that they could "legally" impose the draft in World War II, Korea, and Vietnam.

FDR unlawfully converted the identity of all the people in America to that of "presumed" Territorial and/or Municipal "persons" —- that is, incorporated franchises — and he bilked the National Trust, with the full knowledge and participation of both the British Monarch and the Pope.AfterAfter that, "John Philip Miller" was no longer automatically identified as a man and one of the people, but instead was "interpreted" and "redefined" as an incorporated "franchise entity" engaged in international commerce, and therefore subject to the delegated powers of the so-called Federal Government —- that is, the Territorial and Municipal Interlopers.

In order to pull this off and make excuse for their behavior and suppositions, the plotters had to steal our Trade Names and make this appear to be voluntary on our parts.

They started the planning for this in the 1920s with various "Maternity Acts" that we supposed to apply only to Federal employees and dependents, but which morphed into a census-like recording process of "live births" in each county.

It was harmless enough and unsuspecting people accepted that it was good to have a record of who was born where.

In 1933-34, the innocuous recording of live births was weaponized by the commercial fraud artists as a means of identity theft and unlawful conversion of assets on a national scale. Instead of recording live births, they began registering them— enfranchising each little American baby as an "abandoned" property, "voluntarily" donated to the Territorial State of State as a "ward of the State" by an unwed Mother.

Lately, that wasn't good enough, so the lying bastards reduced the role of the Mother to that of a mere "Informant" — as if our Mothers found us in a garbage can and just brought us into the hospital by chance.

These are our employees, people on our payroll, doing this to us.

They have been doing this since the 1930s and it is with some justification that they look at us like Talking Horses when we object, and they say, "But, this is the way we do it. This is the way we have always done it...." which from their perspective is true. None of the Territorial or Municipal Employees we currently deal with can remember any other system or any other set of "legal presumptions".

So, FDR and Corp just "presumed" that we were all bastard children, abandoned by our

Mothers, left as wards of the Territorial State of State, and the Vermin got away with it because people trusted FDR, though he was acting as their President and in their best interest, and couldn't imagine the evil being plotted against the American States and People by members of the Congress and our sanctimonious International Trustees — the British Monarchs and the Popes, who have always pretended to be our Friends and Allies.

The British Territorial United States thus "seized upon" our Trade Names and hijacked them into their own Territorial jurisdiction in international commerce. This resulted in the creation of a British Territorial Foreign Situs Trust doing business as, for example, "John Philip Miller" and also resulted in the Territorial "State of Ohio" being named as the Beneficiary of his Estate, when he, poor bastard pauper orphan, was "lost at sea" —- which also then resulted in the Municipal United States Government setting up a Cestui Que Vie Trust "in his NAME".

Via this series of mis-characterizations and misrepresentations, our identities and our assets were stolen from us by these organized commercial crime syndicates posing as our own dear government.

As they siphoned away our wealth, the value of our labor, our natural resources, and money, they naturally became more and more powerful, more sanctimonious, and more conceited.

Like their Running Dog, Colonel Mandell-House, they thought they were so very clever that the "livestock" would never catch on.

As Colonel Mandell-House bragged, "not one in a million" would ever know and see through this old, complex, nasty set of lies. And if they did, it would hardly matter, because the "System" would take care of itself.

What we have done thus far is to put a very substantial piece of iron rod in their little red wagon wheels and a boot up their butts. Every American, both Democrat and Republican, should now fully realize that they have been betrayed by members of the Territorial and Municipal Congresses beginning in 1868.

They have been acting in treason since 1868, chiseling and plundering and pillaging the American States and People for a hundred and fifty years, and now, like Prince Philip, they have "retired" to the Commonwealth of Puerto Rico, to "gush and lush" over their bankruptcy protection from the Pope, and what they intend to do to us to reduce our population of "Useless Eaters" and increase their own profits going forward.

I have a different future in view. We reclaim our "reversionary trust interest", act in our declared unincorporated capacity, assemble our State Jural Assemblies, restore our Federal States of States, call a Continental Congress, and seize back all our purloined public and private assets, including our Good Names and Estates.

We keep our heads together and prosecute them as criminals, because that is what they are. We give Notice to all the hired "law enforcement officers" and "agency personnel" that this is what is going on, and we remind them of their duty to uphold the Public Law and respect the rights of their actual Employers.

Meanwhile, we get our own records corrected, join our State Jural Assemblies, hold our elections for our land and soil jurisdiction County Sheriffs, our Justices of the Peace, our Court Recorders, our Coroners, our Public Notaries — and if our Public Servants including the members of the Bar Associations don't come to heel, we have the option of confiscating their property and deporting them, or exercising extradition and hanging them as traitors and international criminals.

For All The Jural Assemblies - 7

Discipline

If you have been doing your homework and following along, you now know how much is riding on the success of the State Jural Assemblies and the willingness and ability of the American People to learn their true and proper role and do the work associated with it.

You are now aware of the gross profit motives of those who have betrayed your National Trust and used and abused the American States and People ever since the Civil War.

You know that the British Monarchs and the Popes have acted in Gross Breach of Trust to allow this abuse.

You know that members of Congress — both Republican and Democrat alike — have deliberately and deceitfully abused your trust, too, and have operated in a criminal conspiracy designed to usurp your power and impoverish you for their own benefit and the benefit of foreign interests.

You know that all these Parties to Fraud and many other crimes have grown rich and powerful at your expense, even the expense of your lives.

And you have reason to know that this has been orchestrated in the same way that any crime syndicate is operated via "patsies" — those who unknowingly contribute their services to evil and via "made men" who know the score and keep the scam running.

Most of us have served as patsies in this scheme at some time or another, simply out of ignorance.

In your fledgling State Jural Assemblies, you will find good solid people who have their heads screwed on tight, who follow the logic and the history, and who study (hard) to get things right. You will also find four other kinds of people: (1) the sincerely confused; (2) disruptors; and (3) disinformation agents; and (4) spies.

Be patient with those who are truly confused and do your best to explain things, even multiple times. Those who have been indoctrinated in the Public Schools run by these monsters have learned and believed lies all their lives and it is difficult for them to "un-learn" all this, all at once. Then, too, much of the fraud involved hinges on words and the use and misuse of words. Not everyone is an English Major, okay? So, it will take time for everyone to completely understand the verbiage and how it was pulled on us.

The Disruptors are all the nasty, pushy, I-am-important-my-issues-count-and-yours-don't, and the "I-have-a-problem-with-that (whatever it is) on a constant basis folks. You all know who I am talking about. They always want to argue and split-hairs and find fault and gripe and blame and do very little to nothing themselves that is constructive, helpful, or correct. They are like little cyclones causing chaos and impeding progress wherever they go, usually babbling about arcane, obscure points of law or grammar or similar ontological, semantic, or religious concerns. They are attention seekers who just won't take no for an answer or allow anyone else a fair shot at addressing other concerns.

Sometimes these characters, especially the paid provocateurs, get together in pairs or small groups, and work together to keep everyone stymied.

Take them aside and explain that people who disrupt the functioning of the Assembly or impede the conduct of business in State Jural Assembly meetings can and will be removed by the Marshal-at-Arms.

Some people are just naturally like this and go from one thing to another seeking attention with no very clear purpose at all, but a substantial percentage of the Disruptors are paid provocateurs engaged for the purpose of causing this kind of interruption and obstruction.

The adoption of some rules of order to conduct meetings can help keep them under control, but occasionally it is necessary to throw them out of a meeting because they persist in disorderly, rude, obstructive behavior. Showing them the door at one meeting does not prevent them from attending again (hopefully in a more thoughtful frame of mind) and it may discourage them from participation at all — but, realistically, their help is that of a flat tire anyway.

Disinformation Agents and Spies are both almost always federal employees or people in trouble with federal authorities who are more or less coerced into infiltrating groups and spreading hokum. This can be any variety of lies or scam operations, but typically involves incitement to violence, baiting to trespass, introduction of illegal goods or contraband, fraudulent fundraising schemes, immoral temptation leading to blackmail, and similar activities.

One good way to provide your State Jural Assembly with a degree of defense from these provocateurs is to "excuse" them before every meeting begins. This is a simple announcement saying, "Anyone who is here under false pretenses, anyone who is working for any foreign government including the Territorial United States or Municipal United States, anyone who is being paid or coerced to be here, must fully disclose their presence and purpose now, or leave the premises."

If they subsequently show up as Federal Witnesses they are discredited for failure to disclose.

Surprisingly, many G-men and women will disclose at this point. They will simply present their badges and tell why they are present and that's that. Most times they will then leave and not come back. If they stay, it's up to you to either ask them to leave or proceed as normal, according to your own best judgment.

I have always practiced a no-holds-barred-look-all-you-like transparency, which discourages these characters from getting all excited and bringing more resources and tricks to bear trying to discover activities that are perfectly lawful anyhow. That said, a State Jural Assembly is by definition a Closed Assembly, meant to be attended only by Qualified Members and known Guests.

Please take a look at the list of typical tricks of the Disinformation Agents and Spies:

1. Incitement to violence. They will come in all red hot and spewing rhetoric and stomping mad or they will wheedle away at your outrage over the theft and injustice aspects of what has been done here. If they can't get people all riled up and "violent" and "insurrectionist" either of those two methods, they will try the "Safety Angle" — and try to make everyone fearful and paranoid, and encourage them to do things like make "contingency plans" as a group, stockpile arms, and take similar actions. They will talk about "getting even" with attorneys and judges and politicians and similar ploys to draw people

into compromising conversations in order to accuse them of threatening Territorial or Municipal government officials.

If you simply step back from their sideshow, and observe where their diatribes and insinuations and topics all lead, it's transparent enough. They are trying to gather evidence that our State Jural Assemblies are: (1) not operating properly, and (2) are "fronts" for "rebels" and "insurrectionists" plotting violent overthrow of the government (such as it is) and/or (3) trying to get people to do or say incriminating things that can be used to accuse them of some form of "terrorism".

Though Americans may justly be outraged, the proper and profitable attitude is to "Keep calm and get even." Or as my Mother described it — "Make like a duck, all calm and unflappable on the outside, paddling like hell underneath."

We all have lawful recourse in answer to their fraud schemes and abuses and have no reason to be afraid or to allow anger to overtake our better sense.

They are the criminals engaged in conspiracy against the Constitutions and against the lawful government of this country — not us. They are the employees caught in gross breach of trust and fraud against their employers — not us. Let them be looking over their shoulders and making contingency plans — not us. And as for our hurts and grudges — criminals seldom have much that can be attached to pay restitution or damages, but in this case, they have amassed vast quantities of credit and goods, homes and lands and pension funds —- all under conditions of fraud and unjust enrichment.

We don't have to resort to violence or worry too much about our recompense. All the Notices have been published worldwide. The Bad Guys, in this case, have no place to escape and the greatest danger we face is our own ignorance.

So when you hear some firebrand ranting and raving and inciting violence and talking "more patriot than patriot" — think twice and think: ah, a possible government agent in our chicken coop — and play your own game instead of his.

Likewise when you encounter a wheedler, constantly moaning and aggrieved about losses and blaming others and whining in an outraged fashion and encouraging in vague terms "doing something about it" — think, ah, a possible government agent trying to drum up business — and again, play your own game.

Ditto the fear-mongers trying to make people afraid of exercising their lawful and natural rights, until they are scared and looking over their shoulders like they are guilty of something for reclaiming their own Good Names and joining their State Jural Assembly.

2. Baiting to Trespass. This is one of the likely results of the "incitement to violence" ploys discussed above, and it is what took down Bruce Doucette and the Colorado Nine.

A Disinformation Agent named Michael R. Hamilton, an insurance adjuster by trade (which should have raised red flags aplenty) insinuated himself and encouraged the people in Colorado to make a tragic mistake.

They mistook the Territorial and Municipal Courts and their Officers for their own "missing" courts and Public Officials.

As a result, they addressed these foreigners as if they were actual County and State employees guilty of malfeasance and dereliction of duty —and they transgressed into the foreign international jurisdiction of the sea and threatened these Officers of the Queen and of the Pope with the punishments that would be owed to actual State (instead of State of State) Officials.

And that is what got them arrested and thrown into jail. Michael R. Hamilton, of course, was nowhere to be seen. He entrapped them using their own ignorance against them and baiting them to trespass.

As a State Jural Assembly member, you have cut your ties to all "federal" entities now in operation and have no cause whatsoever to make threats or transgress into their watery jurisdiction at all.

As irritating as it may be to have their continued operations in your face and to have them operating their private corporations out of your public buildings —don't take the bait.

Realize that you have the means in your hands to correct this situation peaceably —by operating your land and soil jurisdiction States and Counties, by educating the populace, by building up your own Courts to serve the People of your State—-and by exposing their lawless and predatory criminal activities to the proper authorities who are running these corporations on our shores– the President, the Queen, the Pope, the Lord Mayor of London, the United Nations Secretary-General, the various State of State and STATE OF STATE Territorial and Municipal Congressional Delegations, the Joint Chiefs of Staff, etc.

Likewise, don't take the bait when they try to scare you. Make no "contingency plans" and store up no stockpiles of arms, etc., beyond what you may need for your family in some kind of emergency—earthquake, fire, flood, etc.

This is the ploy they used on Schaeffer Cox and his friends in Fairbanks, Alaska. The Federales introduced moles — Disinformation Agents — who were in trouble already on Federal charges, and those men created a climate of fear so that Schaeffer and others were afraid for their lives and "drawn out" to make "contingency plans" and acquire dubious amounts of firearms, etc. under the guidance and entrapment of the same men who were scaring them into these actions and secretly taping the conversations.

Later, of course, this was used to make it look like Schaeffer and the others accused were "dangerous threats" and "terrorists bent on violence" and "unstable" nutcases. They were, in fact, just innocent men being "played" by experts to their own downfall.

Don't take the bait when they try to make you mad, either. When they try to "draw you out" to express anger against judges and attorneys — you can be as enraged as you please — but sit there quiet as a mouse and say nothing. Nothing at all. Let them do all the raging and shouting. Enjoy the show.

3. Introduction of illegal goods and contraband. When the Federales get really desperate, they will get their Agents to bring in contraband — drugs, alcohol, and firearms, but most likely firearms — and attempt to blame you and your State Jural Assembly for "possession" of these items. They will try hard to get you to participate and agree to having these "controlled substances" in your possession or on the premises during your Assembly Meeting.

The original Constitution gives the Federal Government control over Alcohol, Tobacco, and Firearms. This is how and why George Washington got involved in The Whiskey Rebellion. The Federal Government was given control over the sale and transport of these items as a source of income to fund the government.

Since things went astray, they have also helped themselves to "control" over habit-forming drugs, though they have no specific authority to do so, and strictly speaking have no authority over possession or use —- only over "sale and transport" across state lines.

So, look sharp and warn all your members. This was their excuse for Ruby Ridge (rumors of a single sawed-off shotgun) and Waco (rumors of illegal drugs being stored and sold at the Branch Davidian Compound). The shotgun was a "gift" and the drugs were stored by the CIA without the knowledge or help of any Branch Davidian. Go figure. Before Janet Reno unleashed the firebombs and flamethrowers on the helpless women and little children you can still view the FBI footage of the helicopters safely transporting all the drugs out in white plastic bales.

4. Fraudulent Fundraising. The Federales also have control of the US MAIL and United States Postal Service. They love to get organizations involved in illicit fundraising activities by having their agents promote hare-brained Ponzi schemes and membership fraud schemes and unfulfilled product schemes, all of which can land people in jail for a long time and cause a lot of

havoc. Just say no. Any fundraising you do for your State Jural Assembly should be by free donation only, or, if you are prepared to offer a product in exchange for a standard "donation" let it be something like a Veg-O-Matic, not anything produced by the members of your Assembly — no templates for sale, no "Freedom Packages" and so on.

5. Immoral temptation/blackmail. The Federales are famous for using sex and drugs to draw people into compromising situations, filming it all, and using this against the "target" to coerce "cooperation" in any number of situations. Just remember: there are no secrets. Warn your membership that State Jural Assembly members need to conduct their personal lives as if their Mother and the entire Church Choir (or Synagogue School or Mosque Fellowship) were behind one of those two-way mirror windows, watching. Because they are.

That may be an unnerving thought at first, especially if your life up to this point has been "untidy"—but if you want to save your country and your inheritance and live at peace, then keeping your own act clean is really the least of the sacrifices to be made.

Steel yourselves to tell no lies, make no excuses, and to live your lives so that as the saying goes, when your feet hit the floor in the morning, the Devil says, "Oh, no! He's up!" —- or "She's up!" — whichever. Or both, for couples.

And practice saying no, politely, and often.

When you are over one of their targets they will start plying you. Gee, you are such a good fellow! Not like the rest of those, well, unsavory patriots. You understand. You are sophisticated! You enjoy the finer things…. you've gone places (or you want to go places, wherever they might be—actually, the Federal Pen is what they have in mind) and so, yeah, come on, there's going to be this party at the Stag's Leap Inn on Friday, why not come?

At first, the entertainment may be polite and nice. A great dinner party and intelligent conversation, interesting people.

Among those interesting people will be a "Flagger" whose only job there is very closely but unobtrusively observe everything you say and do. In a group of maybe two dozen people, this one will be the one that is always in view, but never actually coming very close to you. Only close enough to hear your conversation using a tiny listening device in their ear. Usually, the Flagger won't be anyone that appears very interesting — probably dumpy and at least middle-aged.

Unknown to you, this is an information gathering event. People will be very interested in you and your ideas and your group — your State Jural Assembly— and since most of them will be beautiful and younger than you, you may be tempted to expound as an elder or merely puff up with pride and brag.

Don't do that. Be modest and keep your opinions very mild. Cream cheese would not melt in your mouth. Play them like they are playing you.

Depending on the issues and their group "take" on you, this business of nice society events may go on for quite a while as they grapple with how to land the fish.

Eat hearty. Enjoy the champagne — but not too much, and don't drink anything that is poured from a fresh bottle. Just absent-mindedly set your glass down somewhere and forget about it as necessary, as many times as necessary.

Eventually, they will figure out what kind of person interests you and try to put you in closer and closer contact with one or more of them. If you are a married man the day will certainly come when someone, perhaps your oldest friend, a mild-mannered bachelor who as already succumbed– suggests, "Why don't you make an excuse? Tell Jill (your wife) that you're going to go to the game with me on Friday?"

And yeah, it will "kinda sorta" be true. It will be a "game" all right, and you will lose—because in most cases the victims don't even know its a game until its over and there's a big "L" painted on their forehead.

These people are experts at this kind of seduction and most likely, you and the members of your fledgling State Jural Assembly, are not.

The best way to go is to warn everyone up front about this kind of slow, attentive, painstaking evaluation and seduction process that the Federales use to entrap good people and turn them upside down, ruin their lives, ruin their marriages, get them fired, steal their patents, nail them on phony tax charges, etc., etc., etc.

Just say no. Practice saying no. Say it politely, but firmly.

And if for some reason you feel that you have to accept an invitation, don't ever let yourself get into a situation where you are dependent and as much as possible, don't go alone. Bring your wife or your husband, your best friend, a couple other Assembly Members. Keep your cell phone. Have a duty driver who is loyal to you. Make sure all sorts of people know where you are going and who will be there. Let nothing at all be secret. Ever.

I regret having to talk about this kind of thing and warn grown people like Mom giving you the business before you go out on a date, but most of the people I know who are members of State Jural Assemblies are good, honest —and unsuspecting— people with no real exposure to the Swamp or Swamp Creatures.

Warn your members and support each other, and remind everyone to keep everything including their own private lives on the up and up.

Be forewarned that you will be getting Swamp Dwellers coming through your doors, because losing their federal contracts is too important an issue for it to be otherwise. They will come and you all will have to be ready for them. Not afraid, not angry — just ready.

People convicted of any serious crime are prohibited from serving as a State Citizen and from holding any Public Office in the actual American Government. They can reclaim their status as State Nationals and live their lives and enjoy their property assets. They can stand on the sidelines and support those who have to carry the torch and operate the States and reconstruct the Federal States of States, but our Forefathers did not intend to have any weak links in our leadership.

Think about that when — as they will — the temptations come to your State Jural Assembly.

You may even be plied with more abstract organization-oriented temptation and attempts to play upon common ignorance. The Federal Agents, however, disguised, may attempt to seduce your State Jural Assembly as a whole.

They will tell you —hey, if you want to be

eligible for "Federal Block Grants" or "HUD and Urban Development Grants" or "Agricultural Loans" or, or, or, then you "have to" incorporate, and "update" and "get modern".

That is exactly what they told all the Counties back in 1965. They didn't explain that all those "Block Grants" would be pittance kickbacks from all the racketeering money the Federales intended to make from taking title to all the land assets of those counties.

They didn't explain that the strength, power, assets, and sovereignty belong only to unincorporated people and unincorporated States and unincorporated Counties, did they?

No, they came in like the Pied Pipers they are, sang a little song and dance, waved piles of cash and tales of more in front of the hungry "locals", told a half-truth or two or three, deflowered some girls, beat up some boys, and poured a lot of drinks —- and before you know it, Joe and Bob and Hank and Rita had signed over everything (even though it wasn't really theirs to sign over) and the Boys from DC were in the Driver's Seat.

If you all fall for that stupidity again, that's where they will stay — and they won't stop until this country and our Ship of State is sunk, because the Swamp Creatures are what they are and have always been.

It's up to you to be wise as serpents and gentle as doves, to politely and with absolute determination cling to your moral principles, to your unincorporated status, to your humble but actual powers, and to your good common sense.

For All The Jural Assemblies - 8

A Nation of Bastards?

I have briefly and simply explained the three basic jurisdictions of law many times before and it was outlined in our book, "You Know Something Is Wrong When….. An American Affidavit of Probable Cause", too.

We live our lives in the Jurisdiction of the Air, before returning whence we came, to the Jurisdiction of the Land and Soil (Earth). In between, our feet tread upon either the land or the sea, which is our choice. It is that choice that concerns us when we are talking about the secular government and the forms of law we encounter day to day— but in order to clear the air:

The law of the Jurisdiction of the Air is divided into ecclesiastical law and canon law, which can loosely be defined as the law for the people who make up the body of the Church (ecclesiastical) and the law for the churchmen and clergy (canon). This in turn relatively reflects the same kind of formula difference as one finds between the Public Law which everyone is supposed to obey and the Private law of the Federal Code, for example.

Ecclesiastical Law is formed of doctrines that are spelled out in the form of Accords and Concords and Creeds and all sorts of Writs and Edicts, while Canon Law is neatly numbered (though voluminous like the Federal Code) and stipulates all the do's and don'ts and rights and obligations and duties of priests and lesser clerics and administrators.

Thus there is a Third Jurisdiction and two more mighty sets of laws and a Christian Assembly that has nothing to do with a secular State Jural Assembly; and, there is a "Divine Government" established by "Assemblies of Believers" known as "Congregations" within a church, but that is not the kind of assembly that we are talking about when we are discussing the American Government (Land) vs. U.S. Government (Sea) and State Jural Assemblies.

Some people are getting this all balled up and confused and someone has to take the initiative to say– whoa!

If you want to argue how many angels can sit on the head of a pin this is not the forum to do that and the State Jural Assemblies are no place to have those kinds of religious discussions. We all have cause to know that although most of our Forefathers were Christian they did not create a Theocracy, nor, for that matter, did they create a Democracy. They instead negotiated for each state to enjoy a "republican form of government" where the power remained solidly based on unincorporated institutions and the free will of the people living on the land and soil of each geographically defined "State".

So the job of the State Jural Assemblies is to organize and re-populate the land and soil jurisdiction of each of the American States, and then, to finish the "reconstruction" of the Federal States of States, so that our Government is restored to its intended form and is fully functional.

That is a big enough job without any religious controversies blurring the lines and making a difficult job even more complex and dragging in issues that have nothing to do with our Secular Government then or now.

Unfortunately, the Roman Catholic Church did poke its nose in and get involved in the Great Fraud in 1925, when it incorporated a non-profit corporation doing business as "the" United States of America (Inc.) in the State of Delaware and continued the same basic scheme as the Scottish Government promoted in 1868 when it created "The United States of America" Incorporated—- naming a corporation after our unincorporated Federation of States and letting confusion and deceitfully similar names promote identity theft, hypothecation of debt, and all the rest of it.

This created a situation where the Holy See had a Territorial Corporation dba "the" United

States of America, Inc., and various Municipal Corporations doing business as the MUNICIPAL CORPORATION OF THE DISTRICT OF COLUMBIA and the MUNICIPALITY OF WASHINGTON, DC, and the UNITED STATES and so on — and the Holy See and its Secular Administration run by the Office of the Roman Pontiff — saw fit to bring along many antiquated and evil practices that it had practiced in Europe for centuries.

These included the Doctrine of Scarcity, the Doctrine of Bastardy, and the practice of Bono Vacantia among other destructive instruments designed to denigrate and invalidate other Christian denominations as well as all other religious faiths— and fleece the populace blind in the name of Jesus.

So although our American Government is and always was thoroughly and determinedly secular in nature and though the Separation of Church and State was very well settled and established in this country prior to 1925, the increasing role of the Roman Catholic Church as a "governmental services provider" thoroughly polluted the administration of both Territorial and Municipal Government Services with religious dogma and prejudice that has contributed mightily to the fraud and abuse that has occurred in our country.

The Order of the Templars came back from the Crusades "infected" with a brand of Gnosticism born of exposure to the more ancient cults of Baal from Babylon and Sumeria, and Osiris from Egypt. The Pope and King Philip of France had also borrowed a great deal of money from the Templars, and were hard up against having to pay them back. So they used the religious differences as an excuse to suppress, murder, and confiscate the property of the Templars.

That is what ultimately created two portions of our modern dilemma — the first being the suppression of the Templars and their beliefs, resulting in Freemasonry and other less savory Secret Societies, and the second being the start of a loathsome habit of the Holy See and its Collaborators of borrowing huge amounts of money from people and then killing off their Priority Creditors.

You can see this most grossly in the Second World War wherein the Holy See and Hitler borrowed huge amounts of money from Jews living in Germany and Eastern Europe, and then, when it was time to pay back the debt, exterminated their Priority Creditors instead. The Municipal corporations under the control of the Holy See and their principal subcontractors — the Alphabet Soup Agencies — were being fully prepared and weaponized to carry out exactly this same maneuver in America, complete with FEMA concentration camps.

This behavior cannot be seen as anything related to religious differences or any misunderstood loyalty to the teachings of Yeshuah. It is criminal behavior — theft, murder, and piracy— motivated by greed and blamed on the victims in every instance since the suppression of the Templars.

The Church attempted to excuse this by adopting what can only be described as doctrinal schizophrenia — preaching the Gospel under the sacred Office of the Pope, and allowing this filthy, violent, horrifying behavior under the Office of the Roman Pontiff. And selling it all under the Church's storefront.

The recent maneuvers have not stopped the problem. The Office of the Roman Pontiff was closed down in 2011, but the "new" Holy Roman Empire started up on its heels and took over the same old function — the Gold, Order, and Dominion function of secretive violence, war-mongering, theft, deceit and criminal brutality. Gold, Order, and Dominion = GOD, and their KINGDOM OF GOD, which is not our Kingdom of Heaven, and not allied with any teaching of Yeshuah.

It is also clear that after bankrupting and liquidating the Municipal UNITED STATES, INC. and granting the perpetrators undeserved bankruptcy protection, the Holy See and its property managers at the Vatican fully intend to simply boot up another deceitfully named Municipal Corporation and reward the criminal members of the Municipal United States "Congress".

That is, after all this, after all the exposure of their misdeeds and criminality, they have learned nothing. They have not turned away from their sins. They have not repented one bit. They have simply coiled around and shed their skin and think that they are going to go right on with business as usual.

My Mother had a good answer for snakes. It's called a garden hoe.

In making these observations it gives me no pleasure to report, nor does the rest of the story, which Kurt Kallenbach explains exhaustively in his publications and on his website, www.kurtisrichardkallenbach.xyz.

The research that Kurt and his team have undertaken coincides, underlines, explains additional — especially theological — history, that only concerns us in that it explains the origins of the ignorant and superstitious practices that have ultimately been elevated to excuse gross crimes against each and every one of us.

Very briefly, clerics at the time of Thomas Aquinas could not explain the nature of the afterbirth that accompanied each child into the world. So they deemed it a live born "human person" that mysteriously died upon entering this world.

We have caught hospital personnel and have hospital records detailing how the afterbirth is seized upon and kept without the knowledge or consent of the Mother or Father, how it is named using our Given Name–purportedly "donated" by the Mother, and how this is used as an excuse to steal and replicate our identity, to create an "infant decedent estate" named after us, and ultimately, to even steal our DNA.

As bizarre as this is, it is true. This has been going on non-stop in Maternity Wards for years and the identity of the Mothers as married women has been being obscured because the Catholic Church refuses to recognize any marriage not given their stamp of approval. Thus, according to them, we are all "bastards" — unclaimed waifs, wards of the State of State, unclaimed property.

One wonders whatever excuse these unrepentant Middlemen can make in view of their sins, for standing as Gatekeepers between the True God and his Children, and as Judges over the rest of us, when they cannot observe the least bit of common decency.

I am sure that the vast majority of Catholics reading this short summation will be horrified and disbelieving, but these bizarre claims and practices are fully and exhaustively proven and documented and they all amount to nothing but a very large pile of lies, half-truths, fantasies, superstitions, and most all — excuses for crime.

As a result, yes, Campers, we find it necessary to even go back and claim our DNA, via a Paramount Claim to our essence from the moment of our conception and the formation of a zygote.

They stole your Given Name and identity. They stole your Earthly estate. They even stole your DNA. All in the "Name of God" and "Jesus Christ", of course.

Repentance must come to this Church — true, lasting, and strictly enforced repentance, because until it does, nobody and nothing on Earth will be safe.

It literally is like nursing a nest of vipers, as their confessions and contrition appear to last all of five minutes before they go do the same evils again and indulge themselves in more lies and half-truths and obfuscations.

Even though our State Jural Assemblies have nothing to do with Congregational Assemblies, and our Courts do not address ecclesiastical or canon law, we do address probate of our estates and our property interests and our intellectual property rights and our private assets —- all of which have been deplorably abused by these hypocrites on a worldwide scale.

Thus it is, that while the British Monarch is responsible for the abuses practiced upon us in the international jurisdiction of the sea, the Pope is responsible for the abuses in the global jurisdiction of the air, and both of them must be held accountable for this state of affairs.

There is a backdoor where religious contro-versy enters in, though it is not a part of our American Government, and is, in fact, a source of gross criminal behavior on the part of sub-contractors run by the Holy See and its Vatican property managers.

As we wake up and get started with the vast house-cleaning and restoration work set before us, it is only rational that all Catholics world-wide object to these gross criminal practices and refuse to support their continuance, the lies against the Mothers and their rights, the lies against the babies and theft of their DNA, their Good Names, and their estates — all of this an-cient, superstitious evil used to excuse criminal activity must stop and it must stop now. It has no validity in fact and certainly has no place in the modern world.

Our State Jural Assemblies have the power and must demand the repeal of Federal Code Title 37, conscripting our doctors, nurses, den-tists, and other health care personnel into the "US" military as "Uniformed Officers" and end the extortionate use of professional licensing to compel them to participate in these bizarre prac-tices and clandestine registrations of afterbirths "as" live born Americans festooned with our Given Names and used to substitute "for" us so as to steal our identities almost from the mo-ment of our birth.

We must all, worldwide, expose these evils and those who practice them inside and outside the Roman Catholic Church.

We must demand that the unrepentant Roman Curia suspend all privileges of incorporation to the members and administrators and Board of Directors of the Municipal United States Congress and not reward these Vermin with any further opportunity to create, organize, operate, direct, share-hold, or benefit from any incorporated entity whatsoever.

They must not be allowed to come back through the door, unroll a new Municipal Charter, and continue on. They must be stopped and they must be punished.

Any attempt to just hand-off the nastiness of the Office of the Roman Pontiff and its profits to a new gang of criminals operating as the "Holy Roman Empire" needs to be stopped in its tracks, too.

We are not a "nation of bastards" and neither are the people of the many other nations of the world which have been denigrated and disserved in the same way, using the same venal practices, the same archaic and evil excuses.

The State Jural Assemblies are therefore reminded that these are not religious issues from the standpoint of the American Government, but they are issues of property crime, false claims in commerce, fraud, conspiracy, unlawful conversion, identity theft, inland piracy, personage, Breach of Trust, copyright infringement, mischaracterization, credit and insurance fraud, bankruptcy fraud, securities fraud, extortion, racketeering, money laundering, kidnapping, treaty violations, and numerous other kinds of crime.

If the Catholics don't voluntarily and honestly clean up their own Church, monitor its behavior, and control its business affairs, it is inevitable that the rest of us will have to expose and embarrass them until they do. It is also apparent that Catholic-owned and operated corporations, like British owned and operated corporations, have embezzled vast amounts of money and resources out of the American States and People and as a reward, have prepared to murder us, their Priority Creditors.

This continued lunatic behavior cannot be tolerated in the modern world, and should rightfully be known and addressed by the State Jural Assemblies going forward—-but not as a religious issue— as a criminal and economic issue.

For All The Jural Assemblies - 9

Grand Theories and "Responses" Debunked

There are many people out there milling around, most of them are well-intentioned and some think they have "the" answer. Some are Disinformation Agents as described in "7 Discipline".

I started life as a mathematician and for me, the numbers have to add up and the logic has to follow through and each quantity has to — at least eventually — be known.

The simple facts are these: (1) our actual government —which we are owed— is not fully operational; (2) it is not functioning as it should because it was never fully restored after the Civil War; (3) we have not restored it, because we were not informed that it needed to be restored— certain parties profited themselves by keeping that obscured; (4) now that we have a grasp of the actual situation, we have the means to restore the government we are owed in our hands and all we need to do, is do it.

Nobody can complain about us taking care of our own business, and there are a great many people worldwide who will feel relieved and reassured that the people of this country finally woke up and are taking control again.

Thomas Deegan and those trying to organize the Oregon State Assembly have gone off the trolley and are advocating a "tear it down to the ground and start over" idea—an insurrectionist anarchist answer—at the same time they are trying to present themselves as the Oregon State Assembly.

Think about this.

How can you pretend to be a member of a State that you are bent on destroying?

Do the words, "shoot yourself in the foot" come to mind? They should.

Thomas Deegan spent two years in jail for trespassing against the Territorial State of West Virginia. He is lucky he didn't get 38 years like Bruce Doucette in Colorado, who basically did the same thing —- all of them against my advice.

Thomas's theories have been tested — repeatedly — and they always have the same result. The patriots espousing these ideas go to jail and the government putting them in jail is not one bit affected or changed for the better.

So. Use your common sense. If you want to change the way things are run around here, you have to do the work of self-governance and assemble your State Jural Assemblies. Act in your unincorporated capacity, take care of business, and tell your employees what you want them to do.

In a similar vein, there are all sorts of Petitions and Arbitrations and other actions being pursued by well-meaning people and groups who are attempting to "move" Congress and/or use principles of law to ensure their immunity.

The Territorial Congress already agreed that you are immune by passing the Foreign Sovereign Immunity Act in 1976. And the Municipal Congress has nothing to say about your immunity, because you are already the "authorized person" associated with all your ACCOUNTS.

Again — think about this.

When you petition a foreign court or a foreign government, you are handing your authority over to them and subjecting yourself to their jurisdiction.

If you are acting as an American, why would you petition the British Monarch about issues that you yourself are supposed to control?

We don't petition their government, which is merely under contract to provide services to our own. We operate our own government and tell them how we want the service they provide to be run.

Do you petition your groundskeeper to mow your lawn, or do you tell him how to mow it?

Get your heads screwed on, organize your State Jural Assembly, and tell your Territorial employees what you want done, and how you want it done.

Then restore your Federal State of State and use it to direct the course of your State's international business affairs — as the Founders intended, instead of abdicating that responsibility and letting the British Monarch and their Territorial Officers act "for" you.

Arbitration of these matters is bound to more or less fail, because the first default is on our side, not the side of either the Territorial or Municipal Governments. We haven't done our part. We haven't assembled our State Jural Assemblies in 150 years. We haven't reconstructed our Federal States of States.

They, the Territorial and Municipal Governments have been left without instructions—hence the claim of a perpetual "State of Emergency".

We have to get busy and give them instructions or the "State of Emergency" continues.

As an additional point on their side of the issue—we already have remedy.

There is nothing stopping us from assembling our State Jural Assemblies, restoring the Federal States of States, and going forward——nothing but our own ignorance about our own government. And sloth, of course.

On an individual basis, there is nothing stopping us from moving our Names and ACCOUNTS back to the land and soil jurisdiction of the States, either. Doing so instantly provides immunity from further presumption against us by either the Territorial or Municipal Governments.

As irritating as it may be in view of the abuses that have gone on, we have always had remedy in our hands and under our control.

This does not mean that we have not been defrauded and suffered Breach of Trust and been the victims of many crimes, because we have, but we must exercise our remedies first before addressing all of that.

Which means — record your decision as the rightful "Authorized Person" to leave Territorial and Municipal Jurisdiction and to return your Good Name and ESTATE back to the land and soil jurisdiction of your State.

Sign the Act of Expatriation from these "presumed" foreign political statuses, re-convey your Trade Name back to permanent domicile on the land and soil of your State, then move all the derivative NAMES back to permanent domicile on the land and soil of your State, too. This process is like re-flagging a ship and moves your "vessels" back to America and back under American Common Law.

Instant immunity, no questions asked.

This is necessary because your Mother was deceived and coerced and mistakenly identified you as a British Territorial Citizen when you were a baby. That is the fact.

Now, as an adult, you have been told about this circumstance.

It is your responsibility to correct the records and declare yourself an American, if, as is to be supposed in most cases, you would rather enjoy your assets and freedom and benefit from the guarantees provided by all the treaties and constitutional agreements—than be counted as a pauper and treated as a debt slave of a British Territorial corporation.

The same is true of the State Jural Assemblies — the States own and are supposed to control all the Federal "State of State" organizations for their benefit, but as we didn't step forward and reorganize and "reconstruct" the Federal States of States after the Civil War, that part and function of our actual government ran amok.

Neither the Territorial nor the Municipal Governments are supposed to be running "State of State" organizations at all.

There is nothing stopping us from finishing the reconstruction of our Federal States of States, taking them out of mothballs, and returning them to full operation — nothing but our own ignorance. Again.

So, no Petitions to members of the Territorial or Municipal Congresses are appropriate (it would be appropriate if we had an actual Federal Continental Congress present to address, but we do not at this time) and no Arbitration of these matters is advised because the default is on our side of the line.

Any knowledgeable Arbitration expert is going to look at this and say— "Well, this appears to be a situation in which you were identified as a British Territorial United States Citizen as a baby, and you have voluntarily remained in that status ever since, so what are you complaining about?"

You can be anywhere you want to be. You can live in Scotland or you can live in France. You can live on the sea or in a houseboat on the Mississippi or you can choose to live on land.

FDR arbitrarily declared that all Americans were to be "presumed" to be out on the sea on holiday, acting in the capacity of British Territorial United States Citizens, and donating all their assets as chattel backing the debts of the local Territorial State of State franchise of the bankrupt Roman Catholic Church non-profit corporation known as the "United States of America, Inc."

It's up to you to declare it bunko and make your other choices known. If you don't want to live on a wrecked boat drifting around out in the middle of the ocean, by all means, forget the Roman holiday and come back home. Ditto the "offer" of British Territorial Citizenship.

It is also up to you to operate your own government and to do so according to the rules your ancestors established until this entire country is awake and organized and educated enough to make other choices.

Finally, there is confusion about what "states" we are talking about. Some people have erroneously identified the Municipal STATE as one and the same as the PEOPLE without realizing that neither have anything to do with us.

The Municipal United States Government runs on the basis of accounts, as in bank accounts. All the various NAMES you see are bank accounts belonging to either incorporated or unincorporated entities.

For example:

"JAMES ALLEN JOHNSON" is a Municipal ESTATE trust bank account belonging to the British Territorial United States Citizen "James Allen Johnson", a franchise of the British Territorial State of Ohio, or, depending on your choice of political status, it can also be interpreted as an ESTATE bank account belonging to the American Tradesman "James Allen Johnson".

"JAMES A. JOHNSON" is a Municipal PUBLIC TRANSMITTING UTILITY bank account that belongs to British Territorial United States Citizen "James A. Johnson" or, depending on your choice of political status, it can also be interpreted as an ACCOUNT belonging to the American "James A. Johnson".

These ACCOUNTS are all "under your name" and you are supposed to know how to operate them, but the Trustees and perpetrators of this whole identity theft and credit fraud scheme neglected to tell you a word about it, much less how to operate these ACCOUNTS.

Nonetheless, bank accounts are what they are, and obviously, a bank ACCOUNT cannot actually own land and PEOPLE cannot actually represent people, either.

So "PEOPLE owns STATE owns LAND" means "Account # 1092-79991-1 owns Account # 51-456902-001 owns Account # 57757779-1-8985030." And there is absolutely no indication in any of that about who owns "PEOPLE"—or at least, pretends to.

These are issues that Donald Trump needs to sort out.

The rest of us have our own hash to settle — beginning with declaring our political status as American State Nationals and explicitly moving our Name and our ACCOUNTS back home to the land and soil jurisdiction of our State, and following up with joining our State Jural Assembly.

For All The Jural Assemblies - 10

Existing Contracts

Once more, this is a discussion that centers basically around the topic of service contracts, treaties, and related issues, but before we go there I want to address for the Second time the pernicious idea that State Jural Assemblies are religious assemblies. They are not religious assemblies.

For starters, if they were religious community assemblies coming to us through the tradition of the English Church such Christian assemblies are called "Congregations" and if coming to us from the Catholic tradition, they would be called "Parishes". Observe that with the single exception of Louisiana, those words are not used anywhere in America to designate any political subdivision.

Second, we all have good cause to know that our Forefathers negotiated a "republican form" of government for our states — not a theocracy, not a democracy, not an oligarchy, and certainly not a monarchy of any kind.

Third, if they had created a Christian theocracy, being a Christian would be a requirement of Citizenship, and of holding Public Office, and of being an Elector. You can see for yourselves that none of this has ever been the case in America.

Fourth, some people have read the book I recommended as a starting point overview, The Excellence of the Common Law, by Brent Winters, and have taken his comments about the Common Law being based on the Bible to an irrational extreme. The "Common" part of "Common Law" is the Old Testament which all three major land jurisdiction religions in the Western World hold in common. That is why our land and soil jurisdiction court buildings have traditionally featured art depicting Moses and the stone tablets of Ten Commandments.

Fifth, if our Forefathers wanted to start a theocracy, the Bible would have been the whole of the law and there would be no other "law" or legislation in evidence. Islam seeks theocracy and has established it in many countries with the result that all law is directly and explicitly taken from the Koran and interpretation of the Koran. If America were ever a Christian theocracy and its government had ever been constructed as such, the Bible would be the only law book in evidence, with many tomes interpreting the Bible for church members (ecclesiastical law) and for church priests and lesser clerics and administrators (canon law). Observe that this is not the case in our courts and never has been.

Sixth, observe that freedom of religion is a fundamental guarantee and precept of our government, which means freedom of belief and practice of religion for all Americans, not just Christians. Faith is a private matter, and the only way it becomes a public matter in America, is if one's faith embraces crime— murder, rape, theft, etc. — which we will prosecute to the fullest extent of the Public Law.

Seventh, we all have cause to know about the Separation of Church and State and the arguments that surrounded it at the time it was adopted, and the same wisdom that ruled our Forefathers then still needs to rule us now.

And this is perhaps an unintended lead-in to the actual topic.

As many of you have noted, the American Government is not a signatory to any modern treaties, memberships, accords, or similar conveyances. Time more or less stopped for us in 1860 with respect to those sorts of things, because the Federal States of States ceased to function. We could have, if we had been properly informed, operated our actual States then as now to resolve the issue — but other parties obscured the facts to profit themselves, and here we are, 150 years later.

So we are not members of the "United Nations". We are not bound by the treaties ending World War I or World War II. We slept through it all. Our largely disloyal subcontractors obligated themselves and pretended to have authority to obligate the American Government to a great many things, all of which are foundationally flawed contracts.

But there are contracts that are not foundationally flawed by fraud and disclosure issues, most of which are now over 200 years old. The most important of these contracts are not the three constitutions creating the subcontracting "federal" government, but are in fact the Peace Treaties that guarantee our peace with the rest of the world and the National Trust indentures of every State and the country as a whole.

The Constitutions are important for the sake of reference points and basic principles, but one must realize that the function of the Constitutions was to set up governmental service agreements. The primary service agreement went to the Confederation of Federal States of States doing business as the States of America. The next service agreement went to the [British] Territorial United States. And the last service agreement went to the Holy See.

Each of these honorable service contracts imposed responsibilities on each of the parties and the granting of "powers" —- basically permission to act and provide the stipulated services— required to enable the recipient of the contract to perform their duty.

This is not unlike hiring a butcher, a baker, and a candlestick-maker. You are giving your "business" to vendors. If a vendor goes out of business or for some reason does not want to contract with you, you have to do the work yourself or find a new vendor.

America is all grown up now and able to provide its own Navy and its own military, administer its own territories, control its own money, set its own trade policies, handle its own patent office, provide its own postal service, and exercise all the other nineteen (19) enumerated "powers" that the States originally handed over to: (1) the Federal Confederacy of States of America; (2) the British Territorial United States; and (3) the Holy See.

Fine enough. In those practical ways it is safe to say that we have outgrown the Constitutions, that the Constitutions have failed to protect us in numerous ways and have been undermined, and so forth—-but it is also true that these pre-existing contracts provide a basis for stability and guarantees that if properly enforced are very beneficial. They also provide a framework for our government that cannot be arbitrarily or thoughtlessly demolished without causing a great deal of destruction and havoc.

For these reasons and because if we wish to have lawful progression and succession and maintain our rightful claims and our National Trusts we must maintain our continuance of government. That is, we can't inherit what our Forefather's provided and handed on to us if we go off willy-nilly. We have to keep our heads and maintain our connection to our past in order to secure our rights and assets for the future.

All of this means that we have to go back, pick up where we left off, restore the government we owe ourselves, and then deal with making changes — whether those changes are service vendor contract changes or fundamental changes to the whole structure of the government we inherited.

Think of the American Government like a grand old Victorian Era house we have inherited. Does it need updating? Of course. Will it still function? Yes.

Do the service vendors we hired to cut the grass and deliver coal to the furnace still owe us Good Faith Services? Yes, they or their successors do.

The cloth-bound electrical wiring and antiquated plumbing need to go. In fact, we may have to tear out and rebuild walls, install new heating systems, and change a roofline or two. No doubt.

We can't just "blink our eyes" and make it so, can we? There is a whole process involved. The inheritance has to be settled and brought forward. The new generation of owners have to take on the responsibilities and deal with the service providers. Then they have to agree on a plan for updates and changes.

It's the same kind of process that we all face now to restore, update, and bring forward our American Government into the modern world.

Educating ourselves, getting our own records corrected, and 'inhabiting" our land and soil jurisdiction States by explicitly re-conveying and permanently domiciling our Names/NAMES back to their jurisdiction — all that is just the first hurdle: reclaiming our inheritance.

Forming up our State Jural Assemblies is the second vital step: taking charge of our house and dealing with the service vendors.

Those who would mislead you into thinking that this is a "free for all" process without a rhyme, reason, logic, or necessity of process, seek only to destroy this country and to provide an excuse for external powers, such as "the UN", to come in here and decide our future "for" us.

That danger and those provocateurs are precisely the reason that we must start where we left off and proceed forward calmly and agreeably and in a business-like manner to restore the government that we both owe ourselves and which the service vendors owe us.

Once our State Jural Assemblies are restored and fully functioning, we can call for our Public

Elections in each State, and elect Deputies to send to a Continental Congress of the land and soil jurisdiction States.

And that— with the actual land and soil jurisdiction States in Congress Assembled and in Session — is where we can make the updates and plan for the changes.

I want to take a moment to explain how we were "Grandfathered In" at the end of the Civil War. This has, obviously, been a problem of Law and Legality, both, for a long time. Provision had to be made to preserve the Inheritance rights to each State National Trust and to the Federal Trust as well.

Those of us who have ancestry going back before 1860 can claim back all rights, properties, assets, and interests of the National Trusts we are heir to, and this is, in terms of Law, what we are doing when we "return home" to the land and soil jurisdiction of our States.

Nobody can say that our States are "abandoned" so long as at least one eligible Inheritor shows up, and thanks to the work we have already done: (1) the Federation Trust has been renewed; (2) each one of the State National Trusts has been renewed and claimed by one or more eligible Inheritors.

This does not mean that these eligible inheritors "own" all the land and soil of say, Louisiana, in their private capacity. It means that they connect the continuity of ownership and right of jurisdiction and inheritance over the land and soil that defines "Louisiana" for themselves and for all other Louisianans.

All it takes is one birthright inheritor in every State who has reclaimed his or her proper political status and identity, and who has ancestors born in the States prior to 1860 to claim back that State's National Trust—-and we have long ago surpassed that threshold requirement thanks to brothers and sisters who were paying attention and taking action three years ago.

And now a few words about the dangers of the Paris Accord that was recently boycotted by President Trump, and which too many traitorous and unauthorized Presidents, Monarchs, and Prime Ministers signed:

The first thing I want to point out to all of you is that most of those persons acting to obligate their countries and people to this insane agreement— which is not, by the way, primarily about "climate change"— are not competent nor authorized to do so.

Like the situation in the "United States", their leaders are not actually "Presidents" of countries, but are instead functioning as "Presidents" or "Prime Ministers", etc., of commercial corporations. The Paris Accords are therefore designed to deceive people into thinking that they and their country have been obligated, when in fact the most that these Fakirs can contribute is the support of their corporations–– either Territorial corporations or Municipal corporations.

It's a another Sting.

It is an attempt by the Holy See to consolidate and control all the organizations providing governmental services at the Territorial level worldwide and to place those corporations under the control of a "Queen".

Via this fraudulent mechanism having nothing to do with the actual countries and peoples of the world, the Pope and the Queen would then control all governmental functions in the international jurisdiction of the sea, and usher in a new age of Commercial Feudalism.

The people in charge of the Territorial service corporations were, for the most part, either deluded or corrupted or just plain gullible enough to vote for this "in behalf of" the presumed shareholders — most of whom don't realize that their identities have been stolen and their natural property rights have been unlawfully converted and that they are "shareholders" at all.

And the motive for all this cooperation and agreement about a carbon tax? Gold. Or to be more exact, access to gold that in fact belongs to the countries and people being defrauded.

This is a long-planned global coup which if

successful, would end all national sovereignty on Earth and hand our countries and our corporations and everything we are and own, over to a multi-national group of Planners.

And who elected them?

And where, wearily, have we heard and seen this song and dance before?

Semiramis, also known as Ashtoreth, Astarte, Isis, Cybele, Columbia (as in District of) and also as "the Mother of all Harlots" and "the Great Abomination" is also called "the Queen of Heaven".

Catholics of the world, is this your Church anymore? The rest of us thought that Mary, the Mother of Jesus, was the only "Queen of Heaven" — at least in the Christian world.

How would they fund this scheme? By their usual means: lies.

By creating a completely bogus and now thoroughly discredited theory that climate change on Earth is caused by excess emissions of carbon dioxide and imposing a horrible, destructive worldwide "carbon tax" — which is just another excuse for continued extortion and piracy.

The Russians, the Chinese, and the Americans are the only ones with the good sense to see through this Sting Operation and label it for what it is — yet another bid of the discredited hierarchy of the Roman Catholic Church to launch yet another "Holy Roman Empire" to the detriment of everyone on Earth.

Catholics — your Pope proposes to play the role of the Anti-Christ, to reboot Satan's Casino using gold stolen from almost every country on Earth, give some gold back to everyone to prime the pump——and use a Great Big Fat Lie justifying a "carbon tax" to pay for it all.

Playing a game of "Good Pope" / "Bad Pontiff" for generations, acting as Middlemen and Gatekeepers in the Spiritual Realm in the same exact way as Bankers have acted as Middlemen and Gatekeepers in the Realm of Commerce —-stealing the Good Names and estates of babies, and assigning these assets to the credit of "deceased" afterbirth debris—then blocking these bogus ACCOUNTS and using our credit and assets as they please, copyrighting our Names as franchises of their corporations, patenting our DNA, selling our labor, taxing us to death for purported "good causes" like the Crusades, and killing for Christ?

It's literally time for all this crappola to end.

You can help by educating yourselves and exposing this gross corruption, and if you are Catholic, you can help by bringing your membership in the Church and your influence with your local priests and bishops to bear. It sincerely gives me no pleasure to bring these ur-

gent and ugly issues to the attention of innocent Catholics worldwide.

I tried to work with the Roman Catholic
Church leadership to put an end to this hideous
nonsense, but —while professing a willingness
to change and make correction with one breath,
they have continued their sins with the next.

You can also help by alerting your local authorities, by correcting your own political status
records, by explicitly making a choice and re-
conveying your Given Name permanently back
to the land and soil jurisdiction of your home
State, and last, but not least, by helping to organize and join your State Jural Assembly— and
operating it according to the guidelines I am
giving you.

Be aware that these are indeed perilous times
we live in, and there is a great deal of urgency
in all of this. Also be aware that your safety and
your property interests depend on reclaiming
your natural birthright political status, operating your lawful State Jural Assemblies, and retaining, for the time being, all the existing contracts, treaties, and conventions that you are
owed.

Don't let anyone cheat you or trick you into
"voluntarily" giving away the protections and the
government you are owed.

For All The Jural Assemblies – 11

"Committees of Safety"

In trying to find guidance in our shared past, many people including myself have diligently researched the practices of the Founders for help going forward. This has resulted in many discoveries and helpful "traditions" coming from many substantially different local County and State Jural Assemblies.

In the eighteenth century communities were much more isolated than they are today and neighbors knew each other in ways and for purposes that are not much in evidence today.

Your neighbor wasn't just someone who lived nearby. Your neighbor's character, skills, knowledge, physical strength, tools and willingness to share all of the above had a direct impact on you and your family's safety and well-being. The exigencies of life in the colonies promoted an awareness of "the Common Good" and the "Public Welfare" that had nothing to do with public assistance checks or food stamps.

In the contentious days prior to the Declaration of Independence, our once-relatively homogeneous communities were split between the Patriots, and the Tories loyal to England. This split caused great social unrest and dis-ease that we can scarcely understand today, and affected people even in their religious practices. Just as the Church of England separated from the Catholic Church over political and social differences, the American Anglican Church was split in half. Patriots became Episcopalians and Tories remained Anglican.

I mention this only to demonstrate how deeply felt and how fundamentally disruptive the Revolution was. Suddenly, there were spies and enemies in every corner. Your dear friends who were Tories no longer spoke to you, and vice versa. People you had known and trusted and depended upon all your life for vital services would no longer do business with you, over the issue of Independence.

It was in this atmosphere in the years leading up to the Revolution that "Committees of Safety" were formed by the Patriots. These Committees served a multitude of functions in all the various communities. They provided an effective spy network to keep tabs not only on what the British were doing, but what their Tory neighbors were doing. They organized assemblies at pubs and in churches and schools and private homes. They established stockpiles of guns and ammunition and food, medical supplies, and tools.

So now we come to a time when, as in the days before the Revolution, people are alarmed about the decayed state of our government and its now-obvious malfunctioning.

Most people have not yet been told the history that got us here, but when they realize that a fundamental part of the Federal Government has been missing for 150 years, they listen up and begin to grasp the seriousness of the situation and also to realize the damage that has been done by those we trusted as our Allies in war and peace: Britain and the Roman Catholic Church.

This Gross Breach of Trust naturally engenders feelings of anger, fear, disorientation, and yes, a certain degree of paranoia. Once again, "Committees of Safety" are forming.

I am not against the principle of having a "Committee of Safety" associated with each State Jural Assembly, but must advise that we are not at war and there is no intention nor need for us to engage in any great struggle other than a mental and spiritual and emotional one.

The Law is firmly on our side of the issues and our jurisdiction; our States and our Federation of States, were never even involved in the Civil War. Our land and soil jurisdiction has been at peace continuously and remains so.

Ignorance of our own history and the fundamentals of law are our greatest enemies.

Neither England nor the Church of Rome want

to fight with us, and as for the respective Territorial and Municipal Governments, they are now largely staffed by other Americans — howbeit, Americans employed by foreign powers — who have no real interest in destroying property in America and fighting with their neighbors.

So the conditions now are fundamentally different than they were prior and during the Revolution and "Committees of Safety" though they may be helpful in organizing and coordinating various kinds of support, including physical support of Jural Assembly members, should not fall into the trap I described in "7 Discipline" as "the Safety Angle".

It is and has long been the practice of Federal Agents, both Territorial and Municipal, to infiltrate Patriot organizations and cause both disruption and to promote various kinds of disinformation. When all else fails, they try to induce a certain brand of paranoia and get people hatching "contingency plans" and stockpiling guns and that sort of thing so as to provide a rational excuse for arresting them. When such moles get extremely desperate, they will also try to introduce contraband — illegal weapons and substances — that they use for the same purpose of providing an excuse for arrests.

It is therefore of the utmost importance to be prudent when organizing a Committee of Safety, and to not entrust its direction to hotheads and gullible people who will reliably fall victim to such intrigues and drag everyone else down with them. It is also necessary to explicitly restrict their activities in behalf of the State Jural Assembly per se.

In most State Jural Assemblies, the security for Assembly functions, meetings, and meeting spaces, is provided by an elected Marshal-at-Arms, with assistance from members of the Committee of Safety. Their duty with respect to the State Jural Assembly is to provide a safe location for meetings, to be prepared to remove disruptive participants, to be aware of any "suspicious" activities (such as bringing in contraband) and to help organize the State Militia.

Please note that the "State Militia" is a different and separate organization from the "State of State Militia", though in fact the members of "State of State Militias" are often confused and think that they are serving their State Militia instead.

State Militias are in fact staffed by members of the State Jural Assembly. Serving in and/or supporting the State Militia is one of the duties and responsibilities of State Jural Assembly membership. Men aged 21 to 45 who are physically fit are expected to join and support the State Militia upon acceptance into the State Jural Assembly. Conscientious Objectors are traditionally allowed to pay a fee in lieu of their Militia Duty, as are women and elders and others who for some physical or mental reason cannot serve.

The American Government at the State-level is set up like the Swiss Government. Every Swiss is trained to use firearms and to serve their community in emergency capacities. They all know basic First Aid. They all belong to Community Safety Brigades. This system is highly effective in promoting Public Safety, reducing crime, and keeping the peace. Jural Assembly Members have the respect and cooperation of local law enforcement and are not viewed as outsiders or threats.

Our land jurisdiction Sheriffs depend upon the Jural Assembly and the Committee of Safety for a ready supply of Deputies when the need arises.

All of this is perfectly normal, lawful, and our unarguable right to organize as part of our right to "peaceably assemble".

The way to view this is that we are being more or less forced to accept the "services" of two very large multinational business conglomerates and they want to make sure that their contracts are renewed, so the nature of their activity is designed to squelch any effort that unfavorably reviews their performance or which seeks to alter the fast-and-loose administration of those services which they have hitherto enjoyed.

And, in the current climate, they are being obliged to compete with each other.

Suddenly, their standard of "service" is being

examined by the people of this country and they are both found lacking. This results in the Territorial Government administered by the Queen (like any business) initiating reforms to "keep their customers" and in the Municipal Government being administered by Municipal Congress trying to keep their slaves, too.

The rest of us, especially members of the State Jural Assemblies, are stuck in the middle playing the role of a Performance Review and Oversight Committee and taking the necessary steps to enforce the contracts we have with these service providers — the Constitutions, as well as addressing the more fundamental issues of finally reconstructing our own Federal States of States and ultimately, preparing for a Continental (Land Jurisdiction) Congress.

Outside of working with the Marshal-at-Arms to secure the meetings and meeting spaces of the State Jural Assemblies and helping with induction of Jurors as members and/or supporters of the actual State Militia, Committees of Safety should not engage in any activities that can be misconstrued as "anti-government" or "violent" or threatening.

Committees of Safety are meant to coordinate the peacekeeping forces of our land and soil jurisdiction States and as we are not at war and have no need nor intention of fighting with our own Territorial or Municipal employees, the best additional use of the Committees of Safety is an educational one. We need outreach to and within the current existing military services and law enforcement agencies.

They need to be apprised of the differences between the "State" and the "States of States" which have been operating on our soil, and they need to be reassured that our peacekeeping forces are intelligently managed and intent on keeping the peace and promoting Public Safety— not fomenting any kind of external controversy or war.

America belongs to Americans. It is our right to act in our natural and birthright capacity, to "accept all gifts and waive all benefits" offered by foreign subcontractors, and to conduct our country's affairs according to the actual stipulations governing it.

Anyone who has any problem with that is obviously in the wrong, and acting on presumptions not in evidence in our Public Records.

For All The Jural Assemblies – 12

Recordkeepers

Amid a lot of deception by others and false accusations against me, I must note that gossip and ignorance are common bedfellows, and are often used to undermine both understanding and progress.

I must also note that the True and Living God despises lies and gossip and always encourages us to overcome our ignorance simply by asking for help: ask to receive and knock to be answered — and feel free to do your own research.

The information I am presenting in this series of articles seeks to fully inform and help guide those organizing their State Jural Assemblies and it is not widely known yet and may still encounter those who, because of their own ignorance or their own concept of self-interest, attempt to deride and discredit things that are simply true.

I have described the overall situation thus:

"The simple facts are these: (1) our actual government —which we are owed— is not fully operational; (2) it is not functioning as it should because it was never fully restored after the Civil

War; (3) we have not restored it, because we were not informed that it needed to be restored— certain parties profited themselves by keeping that obscured; (4) now that we have a grasp of the actual situation, we have the means to restore the government we are owed in our hands and all we need to do, is do it."

I and others have queried a great many experts including the Congressional Research staff, the Librarian of the Library of Congress, the Librarian at West Point, the Librarian at Annapolis, and others recordkeepers of renown and it is fully and conclusively established that:

(1) Most of the Reconstruction Acts are still in full force and effect for the Territorial United States Government; "reconstruction" was never completed;

(2) That the intended Federal Government has three (3) branches, organized as Federal, Municipal, and Territorial — not as we were told in school, Executive, Legislative, and Judicial — which is true, but at another level of organization entirely from the level of organization we need to "reconstruct";

(3) That the American Civil War was never declared by any Congress and was an "executive" action resulting in a commercial mercenary conflict, not a "war";

(4) That the American Civil Conflict was never resolved by any actual peace treaty and that it

could not be resolved by a peace treaty, because it was not a war;

(5) That the Parties engaged in the "American Civil War", whether they knew it or not, were thus acting in a private and commercial capacity;

(6) That all the fisticuffs and bankruptcies and reshuffling that occurred in the wake of the Civil Conflict did not involve the actual American States, but did involve Federal States of States;

(7) That after the Civil Conflict, the original Federal States of States owned and operated by the States, were mothballed as State Land Trusts (in the sense of being owned by the States in charge of the Land and Soil Jurisdiction) doing business as for example, the Ohio State [Trust];

(8) That people in each actual State were coerced without full disclosure by agents of the British Territorial United States to adopt "new" State of State Constitutions;

(9) That the "States of States" thus constituted were British Territorial entities run as franchises of parent commercial corporations in the business of providing governmental services;

(10) That these British Territorial "States of States" have thus been substituted for the Federal States of States that our land and soil jurisdiction States are owed;

(11) That this whole situation has been obscured by those profiting from it and from the deceptive fraud attendant upon it, in terms of facilitating racketeering, political oppression, embezzlement of public funds and private assets, and generally, false claims in commerce ever since;

(12) That the British Monarch obligated by treaty and commercial contract to act as our Trustee "on the High Seas and Navigable Inland Waterways" has acted in Gross Breach of Trust;

(13) That our entire populace has been deceived and mis-characterized, used, and abused as British Territorial Citizens by persons in our employment;

(14) That this has all led to a perpetual "state of emergency", as a fundamental portion of our government has not been operation for 150 years;

(15) That the Municipal Government of the District of Columbia authorized by Article I, Section 8, Clause 17, of The Constitution of the United States, as a "plenary" oligarchy intended to be run by Members of our Federal Congress for the purpose of providing a common meeting ground for our Federal State of States, has instead been run by members of the British Territorial United States Congress and "representatives" of their Territorial States of States;

(16) That these "representatives" have institutionalized this national identity theft and fiscal fraud scheme and benefited themselves from all manner of criminal activity, including the enslavement –on paper– of millions of American for profit;

(17) That these members of the British Territorial United States Congress also acting as members of the Municipal United States Congress have abused and misinterpreted their "plenary powers" to operate Municipal STATE OF STATE organizations and to incorporate municipal franchises far outside the authorized limitations of the geographic "ten miles square" of the District of Columbia;

(18) That our unincorporated Federation of States doing business as "The United States of America" since September 9, 1776, suffered identity theft by commercial corporations using deceptively similar names: "The United States of America, Incorporated" (Scotland, 1868) and the "United States of America, Incorporated" (Delaware, Roman Catholic Non-Profit, 1925) and that this process of identity theft has continued and expanded to include Municipal Corporations like the UNITED STATES and the USA;

(19) That this has all resulted in gross criminal activity including the hypothecation of debt, the issuance of false property titles, the falsification and substitution of lawful records for le-

gal registrations, the illegal and immoral securitization of living people and their assets resulting in enslavement and peonage being practiced in the modern age, and many, many other evils all contrary to the treaties and contracts that this country is in fact owed;

(20) That this, in turn, has enriched the perpetrators of these schemes to an unbelievably inordinate degree and that they have used this wealth to promote the development of the same corruption in other countries via the abusive operation of Territorial and Municipal "Service Corporations" against the Countries and the People that employ them and which they are supposed to serve in Good Faith;

(21) That we have remedy for this situation by calling the actual States to Assemble, which is done by people operating in their natural unincorporated birthright capacity (instead of as "persons" obligated to act as franchises of the guilty corporations involved);

(22) That State Jural Assemblies embody each State;

(23) That these land and soil jurisdiction States, in fact, own all these corporations or are owed the control of them as their actual employers;

(24) That the perpetrators of these crimes and conspiracies against the actual government of this county and against our Constitution(s)

have been Notified and instructed to make correction;

(25) That they have not chosen to do so and continue to run amok, except that the British Territorial United States has bowed somewhat to the inevitability of the moral imperative to serve their employers;

(26) That we, Americans, born on the land and soil of our States, have every right to assemble in whatever capacity and whenever we choose to do so;

(27) That we, the American States and People, are owed a great deal of money and credit and the return of the control of all our "borrowed" assets;

(28) That we have not knowing, willingly, or voluntarily entered the foreign jurisdiction of either the British Territorial United States or the Municipal United States and that a well-orchestrated and organized mechanism of unconscionable entrapment has been used to mis-characterize us all as British Territorial Citizens or Municipal CITIZENS and literally to substitute incorporated entities — using the "infant decedent estate" scam— for living Americans;

(29) That in order for our Government to be fully operational and functioning as intended, we must correct and rebut these deliberately created false legal presumptions being held against our States and our People in Breach of Trust;

(30) That we have every right, reason, and need to promptly address these matters as international crimes and treaty violations, and that we also have every right, reason, and need to form our State Jural Assemblies, operate our government, restore our Federal States of States, require Good Faith Service performance from our employees, and get on with our lives with a minimal amount of continued interference from criminals and fools.

Anyone, anywhere who thinks that they have evidence disproving one iota of what I have presented is welcome to come forward and try to argue against the Public Records and the observable circumstance, the Congressional Research Staff, hundreds of historians, and thousands of public records.

Any misbegotten idea that "I" am the "problem" or that I am misleading anyone about this needs to be promptly dispensed with.

And now to the more limited but necessary consideration of keeping the records of State Jural Assemblies.

Each State Jural Assembly needs to elect a Recorder, whose functions may include keeping "minutes" and tape recordings of Assembly Meetings initially, though it is to be hoped that a Secretary will soon be engaged to undertake those tasks and leave the Recorder free to do only actual Recording functions

Records are by definition all the paperwork associated with actual land and actual soil and actual people.

Registrations apply only to legal fictions — corporations — that hold charters granted to them in some form by the State of State or STATE OF STATE organizations and are meant to apply only to the "citizens" and dependents — Territorial Citizens and Municipal CITIZENS of the British Territorial Government and the Municipal United States Government— working and living temporarily as "residents" on our shores.

For those of you now reading this who are recalling all the "registration" processes you have undergone, you will now realize that you were "deemed" to be operating in the capacity of such a "citizen" or as an actual incorporated entity when you did so: vehicle registrations, birth registrations, voter registrations, registration of "Selective Service" applications, and so on, are all foreign to us and our land jurisdiction States and our People — and are all executed in the international jurisdiction of the sea.

So, obviously, your State Jural Assembly needs to have a Recorder, not a Registrar, and the primary duty of that Office needs to be keeping Records related to the Jural Assembly and its Members in order and secure.

Membership Records are confidential for the

most part and only the names and addresses of the Jural Assembly Members are generally available.

Remember that in "re-populating" your soil and land jurisdiction State, you need not become a member of the State Jural Assembly. You are welcome to function as a State National and have no obligation beyond keeping the peace and obeying the Public Law.

Remember also that in choosing to become a State Jural Assembly Member you are operating —at least temporarily and successively, a Public Office — that of "Juror", and as a Juror, you are considered to be a "State Citizen" in addition to being a "State National" while serving "Jury Duty".

Remember finally that the Officers you elect within the State Jural Assembly are accepting considerably more and different obligations than just serving as a Juror. Sheriffs and their Deputies typically serve in "on duty" and "off duty" shifts and on an "as needed" basis. Judges and Coroners serve pretty much 24 hours and seven days a week and may be rousted out of bed at odd hours, required to travel within the State, etc, Recorders like Sheriffs and Deputies enjoy more regular hours and schedules of "duty" which at the start of the Jural Assembly process are more or less loose and as necessary.

The State Recorder function is vital. It creates and preserves the Public and Private Records upon which the legitimacy and proof of the proper functioning of the Jural Assembly depend. Protecting the Person and the Records of the State Jural Assembly Recorder are therefore important considerations, and securing the Records in multiple copies and in multiple locations is also necessary.

Ideally, all Records are created in original triplicate at the time of their creation, with one copy going to the Jural Assembly Member, one going to the soil jurisdiction County level organization, and one remaining with the State Jural Assembly Recorder. Realistically, at the beginning, we are all dealing with less than ideal circumstances and photocopies of documents may have to be accepted instead.

The necessity is to provide proof of Due Diligence when operating our State Jural Assemblies.

We need to qualify our Jurors which includes the documentation and declarations already discussed — a Birth Certificate or similar public or private record showing when and where a man or woman was born, two Witnesses affirming the identity of Jural Assembly candidate, Act of Expatriation from Territorial or Municipal citizenship, Acknowledgement, Acceptance, and Re-Conveyance / Declaration of Permanent Domicile of our Given Names back to the land and soil of our respective States of the Union, Certificates of Assumed Name also removing their NAMES back to permanent domicile on the land and soil of the State, and a signed and witnessed Mission Statement/Jural Assembly Membership Agreement of the kind I provided as an example.

This creates a Record of the Origin of the Jural Assembly Member on American soil, a verification of their living identity by people who know them, and the rest of the documentation clearly demonstrates their intention to return home to the land and soil jurisdiction and to operate in their unincorporated capacity as one of the "people" and not as a "person".

This "package" is necessary to prove that the Juror is qualified to serve as a Juror of the State Jural Assembly, that the Juror is cognizant and freely choosing the capacity in which they are operating, which in turn validates the actions of the Jural Assembly as a whole.

The Recordkeepers are responsible for collecting, securing, and distributing this information as needed. Typically, the Juror will receive back a complete copy stamped by the Recorder, one copy will be kept by the State Jural Assembly, and one kept for the County Recorder.

Committee of Safety members should have access to this information on an as needed basis and may maintain an active secure digital database.

To an extent, all of this is to be treated as public information pertaining to someone holding a public office, without unduly disclosing or publishing anyone's confidential data. For example, It may be necessary for candidate Jurors to show the Recorder a verified Birth Certificate to establish their place of birth or to produce other family-related documents, and for the Recorder to keep a black and white copy, but it is at no time desirable for a Recorder to unnecessarily divulge details obtained from such records or to keep original records. The Recorder should stamp the package as complete, scan it, distribute the copies, and secure the copies left in his or her possession.

Records of times, dates, quorums, meeting minutes and similar documentary evidence in support of the State Jural Assembly's activities should also be maintained both by the Recording Secretary and by the Recorder's Office.

Hopefully soon a complete understanding of the situation on the part of Territorial and Municipal Employees will lead to vastly increased cooperation as they wake up, too, and realize that we are not upstart insurrectionists or competitors for their jobs, but are and have always been their employers exercising rights, responsibilities and duties that have always been ours.

Such a peaceful resolution and understanding should lead to more cross-communication and cooperation and assistance becoming available from Territorial and Municipal personnel.

For example, Travel Cards are appropriate to issue to Jural Assembly Members and others who have chosen to reclaim their State National status, instead of Driver Licenses. Likewise, Regulation Z stamps can be issued to identify private cars and trucks in lieu of registration stamps. Whether we do this for ourselves or instruct our employees to do it for us, these distinctions need to be made, and these services need to be made readily available without any suspicion, coercion, or obstruction by Territorial or Municipal employees.

The Recorders together with Recording Secretaries and Public Notaries elected, trained, and confirmed in Office by the actual State Jural Assembly together make up a team that evidences, secures, and officially affirms our political status, our identity, the capacity in which we are choosing to act, and which ultimately secures the peace and the proper functioning of the State Jural Assemblies and the country as a whole.

For All The Jural Assemblies – 13

Judges, Justices, and Hired Jurists / Judge Anna Blows the Whistle on the Whistleblowers

Imagine an apple. The apple has a skin, and inside the skin, it has sweet juicy flesh. You can't get to the flesh without piercing the skin.

It is the same way with the land and soil jurisdiction we are heir to.

The "soil" is the top six inches of the land, like the skin on the apple.

All the rest deeper than six inches is "land" — the flesh of the apple.

By definitions long established, the soil comprises the National Jurisdiction of the States, and is managed by our unincorporated Counties.

The land comprises the International Land Jurisdiction of the States and is managed by our unincorporated State Jural Assemblies.

Land and soil are inextricably bonded together, like the skin and flesh of an apple. That is why we speak of "the land and soil" of Wisconsin or Virginia or Texas.

That is why when you become a State Jural Assembly Member, the County Jural Assembly is also created, and vice-versa.

Our Ancestors were determined that no king or government was going to control their lives again, so they made the County– the skin of the apple — the fundamental political unit and supreme political jurisdiction in the American Government.

Strange but true, the County Sheriff elected by the County Jural Assembly Members is the top Public Law Official in the country. Within the physical boundaries of his County, he is the embodiment of the Public Law and its chief enforcer.

Because he works for the soil jurisdiction, the actual County Sheriff is a "Peacekeeping Official" and not a "Law Enforcement Officer". See the difference?

Peacekeepers work for the people, the land and the soil. Law Enforcement Officers work for "persons" — the corporations and their shareholders operating as incorporated States of State, like the "State of Ohio".

We have been well and thoroughly confused and duped into thinking that their "County Sheriff" is our "County Sheriff", when in fact an unlawful conversion has taken place.

Many of those operating our Counties back in the 1960s took the bait of "Federal Block Grants" and elected to incorporate the unincorporated Counties they were working for.

In doing so, they unwittingly removed and converted the actual County Government into mere commercial corporations operated as franchises — like Dairy Queen franchises of Territorial and Municipal corporations.

They handed over our sovereignty "for us" in exchange for racketeering kickbacks.

Ironically, we are fortunate that those same people who voted for the unlawful conversion of the Counties were already unwittingly functioning as incorporated "persons", so had no authority to give away our Counties. They were merely employees of ours.

They had already "vacated" their natural capacity as unincorporated Jurors.

Many Counties tried to have it both ways and kept the unincorporated County running and simply set up a corporation calling itself something similar — like, "The County of Jackson" instead of "Jackson County", so that the offered federal kickbacks could be laundered through "The County of Jackson".

This set up a situation where County Officials were, for a time — and some still are— operating in two separate capacities. The Sheriff elected to the unincorporated soil jurisdiction office simply put on a different hat as the occasion demanded, and functioned as the "Sheriff" of the incorporated "County", too.

But our ancestors set it up so that no man can serve two masters.

The problem is that our actual Counties are political subdivisions of our States and they occupy an entirely different jurisdiction — that of the land and soil — which does not recognize or tolerate any form of "Dual Citizenship" at all.

The land and soil jurisdiction of this country does not allow us to operate in incorporated and unincorporated capacity at the same time. It's one way or the other.

Either you operate as the actual Sheriff of the unincorporated County and State, or you operate as a "Sheriff" of an incorporated "County" franchise of a State of State. See the difference?

There is a Macon County Sheriff working for Georgia, the actual State, and then, out of the blue, there's suddenly a "County of Macon" and the "Sheriff" of the "County of Macon" is working for the [Territorial] "State of Georgia", instead.

Sleight of hand. Presto-Change-O! One minute you are standing on the land and soil and your County Sheriff is your County Sheriff, and the next he is a patsy working for a foreign corporation. Go figure.

In the years since all that happened, things have gotten even more balled up, and we've added another layer of this incorporation scam. Instead of working for the Territorial State of State, the man who appears to be working as your County Sheriff may be working for a Municipal STATE OF STATE corporation, instead.

These moonlighting "Sheriffs" and other "County" Officials are –for the most part unwittingly — functioning as impostors — appearing to be land and soil jurisdiction County Sheriffs and County Officials, when in fact they are being paid by foreign corporations and not standing on the land and soil jurisdiction of this country at all.

And this explanation actually does pertain to the main topic, which is Judges, Justices, and Hired Jurists.

All the people you see inhabiting what appear to be your Courts are Hired Jurists, and they will admit it.

Go ahead and ask them. Walk up to any of the State of State Judges or Municipal STATE OF STATE Judges and ask them the question: "Are you a Hired Jurist?" —- and they will tell you, why, yes, I am.

They will be surprised that you asked, but

the vast majority will answer truthfully.

The same scams and unlawful conversions that I just described with the County Sheriffs apply to the Judges, Justices, and Hired Jurists, too.

99.9% of the members of the Bar Associations are not qualified to act as actual Judges or as Justices, either one.

In the course of the long researches that led up to this moment, we surveyed the "Judges" operating in both the Territorial States of States and the Municipal STATES OF STATES courts, and out of approximately ten thousand of these Hired Jurists, we found one (1) guy in Wisconsin who was actually qualified to act as an actual Judge in a Public Court—- if and when he elects to reclaim his natural and unincorporated status as a Member of the Wisconsin Jural Assembly.

The rest of these people are just Hired Guns, working in private quasi-military and private corporation tribunals.

Instead of being employed by the actual unincorporated State or County as actual Judges and actual Justices,, they were suddenly reduced to the capacity of being Hired Jurists in the employ of foreign corporations doing business as either Territorial States of States Courts or Municipal STATES OF STATES COURTS.

The California Courts ceased to function and the incorporated Territorial State of California Courts and the incorporated Municipal STATE OF STATE COURTS took over the "Judicial Functions"—- but the actual unincorporated Courts owed to the People of California and the people of each County in California, disappeared. Overnight.

And that is why you can't find justice in this country anymore.

Both the Territorial State of State and the Municipal STATE OF STATE are for-profit organizations in the business of providing governmental services. The service they are providing tends to be racketeering aimed at fleecing the actual living people out of their assets for the benefit of their respective corporations.

And their Hired Jurists, are, after all, working for them, and not occupying any Public Office — - so what the hey?

They get away with what they can get away with.

I had a moment of supreme irony the other day. One of my supporters was trying to explain why I am not a member of the Bar Association in Alaska and why in fact I couldn't be a member of the Bar and serve in the capacity that I am serving.

He made the error of describing me as a "common law jurist", as if I were a Hired Jurist — only operating a common law court like counterparts in the State of Alaska are operating commercial corporation courts.

Closer, but still no banana.

The Alaska Statehood Compact created a "National Trust" for Alaska operated as the Alaska State. That National Trust contains the land and soil jurisdiction of Alaska, even if Alaska has not yet been formally enrolled as a State in the Union. Therefore, I, as one of the People of this country, can invoke and fill the empty Public Office of Alaska State Judge or Justice or Justice of the Peace (at the County level).

When we realized the scam being played our research led us to the old Government Land Office and the discovery that although Counties were mapped out and designated in Alaska at the time of Statehood, the land and soil jurisdiction of the State were never occupied. In a sense, our State did not exist, except as a National Trust laid out on paper.

It was up to us to choose to act in our unincorporated capacity as County and State Jural Assembly Members, to occupy our State and our County, to hold our elections and conduct our business as the lawful Inheritors of the National Trust and the land and soil jurisdiction owed to Alaska and Alaskans.

There were only a dozen or so of us up to speed to begin with, so it was a matter of staring at each other in disbelief, going through the motions, and everyone electing each other to different land and soil jurisdiction Public Offices, all of us serving as State Citizens.

Fortunately, it doesn't matter how many or how few qualified State Jural Assembly Members there are for the land and soil jurisdiction to be occupied. Even one (1) qualified Elector operating in their unincorporated capacity prevents the corporations from claiming "exclusive legislative" control — a condition that would leave us with no land and soil jurisdiction to stand upon and result in the collapse of our country and our States.

I filled the Public Office of Alaska State Superior Court Judge. See the difference? Alaska State Superior Court Judge —- not "State of Alaska" Superior Court Judge.

"Alaska" and the "Alaska State" National Trust were not "abandoned" and no "exclusive legislative" hegemony was achieved by the usurping commercial corporations as a result.

The actual State and People have survived by the skin of their teeth, much to the consternation and annoyance of the foreign commercial corporations that have labored so long and so hard to take over our country, steal our resources, and enslave our people for their profit.

At the County level, the people are served by "Justices of the Peace". At the State level, the people are also served by "Justices" as in "Justices of the Supreme Court". Also at the State level, because not all of the State's international jurisdiction was ever delegated away, we have "Judges".

All the "persons" are served by Hired Jurists arbitrarily calling themselves "Judges" or "Justices", none of whom are holding any valid Public Office in the American Government at all.

So the additional irony is that I am an actual Judge holding an actual elected Public Office approved by the people of this State, and I am the one being accused of "lying" and being a "fake Judge".

There are some people who are so stupid or so evilly anti-American, that they can't note the difference between "Ohio", "Ohio State", "State of Ohio" and "STATE OF OHIO", even when you point it out and explain the difference to them.

The fact that there are, as a result of these different entities —- both unincorporated and incorporated —- multiple court systems in play, also passes them by.

Obviously, too, those who work for these foreign corporations and whose jobs depend upon them, are motivated to continue this scam and this effort to undermine the people and their government, just as the living people have an interest (once they are alerted to it) to regain their unincorporated status.

I am willfully serving the People of Alaska, instead of the Persons of Alaska.

The reason that I have not been arrested and charged with "impersonating a Judge" is that those who would have to bring the charges are in fact impersonating our Judges — and as Hired Jurists, they know it.

Strange and incredible as it may seem, I'm not the Fake Judge here. They are. Just as our elected County Sheriffs are the actual Sheriffs and their "Sheriffs" are just stand-ins, calling themselves "Sheriffs" but acting in completely different and foreign capacities.

Now, with all of this in view, listen to this clap-trap from the "Southern Poverty Law Center" —- which I have famously observed is not "Southern" has nothing to do with "Poverty" and is a "Legal" Center having nothing to do with the actual Public Law — and you will see what we are up against, both in terms of

bare-faced lies and misrepresentations and in terms of vicious self-interest on the part of these groupies feeding off the corporate court system.

http://thewhistleblowers.info/warning-anna-maria-riezinger.../

Please also note the deliberate mis-characterization of me as a "Sovereign Citizen"—- which is a meaningless oxymoron. It is impossible to be a "Citizen" and a "Sovereign" at the same time, thus these ignorant people — who are claiming to be experts in the "Law" while offering "Legal Services", continue to act as Ignoramuses and to mislead people so as to prevent them from knowing and exercising their true power as State Jural Assembly Members.

And thus also prevent us from restoring the government we are owed and keep us from acting in our natural capacities and seek to usurp our Public Offices and replace them with employees of their foreign, for-profit "governmental services corporations" instead.

Wise as serpents and gentle as doves, folks. The ignorance we are surrounded within the general populace is thick enough to cut with a knife. The guile and evil of the men actually "in the know" who are orchestrating all this is also not to be underestimated.

Once you know who you are and how your actual government is supposed to operate– and in which jurisdiction your actual government exists, you will realize how we have all been played and what you have to do to correct it.

Reclaim your natural unincorporated political status, re-populate your unincorporated land and soil jurisdiction State, and, as members of the

State Jural Assembly, occupy your "vacated" actual Public Offices —- including the County Justices of the Peace, the State Justices and the State Judges.

I guarantee that the phonies working as Hired Jurists won't have a word to say about it.

For All The Jural Assemblies – 14

Sheriffs, Militias, and Marshals

In our earlier discussion about "Committees of Safety" we discussed the issue of Sheriffs and the fact that there are two different kinds of Sheriffs — those who are public Peacekeeping Officials and those who are private Law Enforcement Officers (LEOs)—-hired guns to go with Hired Jurists, though most LEO's don't realize this and are working in the dark.

Notice the difference in terminology? Officials versus Officers?

The actual public officials who are Sheriffs occupy the land and soil jurisdiction of the States.

The corporate "Sheriffs" naturally occupy offices in the "County" Corporations, all operating in the international jurisdiction of the sea— and all being entities of the same kind and status as Dairy Queen, howbeit in the business of providing "governmental services".

A land jurisdiction Sheriff functioning in actual Public Office in say, Clayton County, Ohio, is the highest ranking law official in the County, bar none. Nobody outranks them. Not the District Attorney. Not even the Governor of the State outranks an actual County Sheriff on his home turf, and certainly, neither does the Governor of any "State of State" outrank a County Sheriff. Anyone working as a "Sheriff" for any incorporated entity is a lot farther down the totem pole, too.

Peacekeeping Officials of the actual land and soil jurisdiction (unincorporated) Counties outrank Law Enforcement Officers hired by incorporated "Counties" by many orders of magnitude.

The actual County Sheriff is responsible for the enforcement of the Public and Organic Law, including the actual Constitution owed to our States and the protection of the property, persons, and guaranteed rights of the people living within the borders of his County.

He only acquires his god-like powers when there is an active, qualified State Jural Assembly present in the State, and at least a few qualifying Jurors in his County to elect him. There is no exact quorum required for these County Sheriff elections, but the more people who realize the importance of joining the State Jural Assembly and thereby also "re-populating" their County, the better.

I look forward to a day when all Americans fully realize how close we have come to losing our country. I also look forward to the day when the People put aside the shackles they have been living under and realize the blessings of being free again. There won't be any arguments anymore about political status. There will be a stampede of those leaving the "US" and coming home to America.

So those County Sheriffs who are Peacekeeping Officials serving the unincorporated land and soil jurisdiction Counties, are the embodiment of the Public Law and the executors of the Law of the Land and the Law of the Soil within their County's borders.

All "Sheriffs" serving incorporated "Counties" as Law Enforcement Officers are obligated to come to the aid and assistance of the actual Sheriff and to obey the directions of the actual County Sheriff.

People sometimes try to make sense of this by characterizing one or the other of these different kinds of "Sheriff" in terms of being "elected" or not, but in fact, both are elected.

The actual County Sheriff is elected by County Jural Assembly Members, who are also automatically State Jural Assembly Members and vice versa.

The Corporate Sheriff is also "elected" but he is elected by corporation shareholders and employees who are registered to vote in the private elections of the foreign [Territorial] State of State, Inc. or even the Municipal STATE OF STATE, INC.

These are two completely different kinds of "Sheriff" acting in two separate jurisdictions and two completely different capacities. One is a Public Peacekeeping Official and one is a private corporate employee working as a "Law Enforcement Officer".

Some LEO Sheriffs try their best to uphold both the Public and Organic Law of the actual County and the private "statutory law" that rules the Public Policies of the foreign corporations they work for. Sheriff Richard Mack is a good example of a LEO faithfully struggling to also fulfill the "vacated" Public Peacekeeping duty of the actual County Sheriff. His epic battle, Mack and Prinz v. USA, Inc. is a testament to two Americans who did their best with a bad situation.

That said, it has been a hard paddle swimming against the tide, as millions of unwary Americans were conscripted and "converted" without their knowledge or consent from being State Jural Assembly Members and State Electors, into functioning as mere private Shareholders in a bankrupt foreign corporation.

Fortunately for us, all these non-disclosed attempts to give away our inheritance and sovereignty "for" us by our disloyal and often clueless employees have been tainted by fraud and fraud knows no statute of limitations.

Law Enforcement Officers (LEOs) as employees of private, for-profit, foreign corporations are allowed to be here and to function under what are known as "Private Security" or "Pinkerton" Laws and have the same exact authority as a Floorwalker at Wallmart, except when their activities involve directly protecting the U.S. Mail, infrastructure related to the U.S. Mail (Post Offices, Post Boxes, etc.) or the Railroads and their infrastructure— tracks, stations, crossing lights, etc. Then they take on the character, but not the office, of Federal Marshals, and employ the same kind of "armed authority" as Federal Agents working for BATF, FBI, etc.

Actual State Militias are not the same as State of State Militias.

State Militias are manned by State Citizens who are members of the State Jural Assembly. Similar to the system of the Swiss Cantons, their focus is community safety and preparedness on a statewide basis. Members are taught firearms safety, marksmanship, first aid, and train in one or more specialties. In the event of attack or natural disaster, the State Militia Commanders can call upon one or more County Militias for assistance. They can also call upon the "State of State" Militias, the State of State "National Guard" and the local U.S. Military Commanders for assistance.

State of State Militias including the State of State "National Guard" are quasi-military or paramilitary organizations manned by State of

State (Territorial) U.S. Citizens who are corporate shareholders and enfranchised voters.

The actual State may employ additional peacekeeping Public Safety Officers, whose duty is to uphold the Public and Organic Law in places and in situations where the people of the State (State Nationals) need protection or assistance. These local State peacekeeping forces have traditionally gone by a variety of names — Troopers and Rangers, for example.

Like their counterparts, these men and women derive their authority directly from the State Jural Assembly and while on State land, they traditionally have absolute peacekeeping authority over everyone but the County Sheriff and in some States, the State Militia Commander.

The Authority Pyramid in the actual American States goes like this:

County Sheriff (Peacekeeper- Public)

State Marshal-at-Arms (Peacekeeper – Public)

State Militia Commander (Peacekeeper- Public)

State Troopers or Rangers (Peacekeeper – Public)

LEO's – Private Pinkertons, "Sheriffs" (Law Enforcement – Private)

Private Detectives, Bailiffs, etc. (Can be State or State of State)

And on the Federal (International) side:

Federal, also known as Continental, Marshals (Peacekeeper- Public)

U.S. Marshals (Law Enforcement – Private)

Agency Personnel (Law Enforcement- Private)

Provost Marshal (Should be a Peacekeeping Officer, but isn't currently.)

It must be understood that the authority these officials and officers have depends upon "where they stand". On the land and soil of the States, actual County Sheriffs and State Troopers and Federal Continental Marshals outrank all LEO's and Agency Personnel.

Federal Marshals serve in "Districts" defined by Postal Service Districts, sometimes called "Postal Service Areas" in an attempt to avoid confusion with other kinds of Federal Government "Districts" such as "Judicial Districts" and "Military Districts". These Postal Districts often overlap several States and create one "Service District" ruled over by one Federal Marshal and as many Deputies as needed.

Actual Federal Marshals are International Land Jurisdiction Officials who are supposed to be operating under the auspices of the unincorporated Federation of States, dba, The United States of America. Their job is to coordinate efforts to intercept, prevent, and prosecute crimes peculiar to interstate/international land jurisdiction venues, including the trafficking of people and contraband, kidnapping, bank robberies, train robberies, mail fraud, consumer crimes, securitization scams, and much more.

Federal Marshals work with counterparts operating in the International Jurisdiction of the Sea who are corporate employees known as "United States Marshals" or "U.S. Marshals". These sea-going Marshals then also interface with the Coast Guard, INS, Border Patrol, FBI, etc. to coordinate efforts to detect, prevent, and prosecute crimes of inland piracy, false conversion, smuggling, international mail fraud, human trafficking across national boundaries, kidnapping, bank securities transfer schemes, drug running, and so on.

The designation "Federal" goes back to the "Federation of States" that the "Federal Marshals" work for, but without our State Jural Assemblies and people knowledgeably functioning as State Citizens, the Federation has also been "de-populated" and forced to exist on fumes and volunteers. This has meant that half of our protection in international jurisdiction has been undermined for lack of our State Jural Assemblies being in full and competent operation, and that empty spot in our law enforcement shield has invited many abuses and a proliferation of crimes in specifically these grossly understaffed positions.

To add to the confusion, the U.S. Marshals have started calling themselves "Federal Marshals" — which they are not.

Similar to the case of the actual County Sheriff vs. the Corporate LEO Sheriffs, the actual Federal Marshals are Peacekeeping Officials, not Law Enforcement Officers. They work for the Federation of States, not "federal" Territorial or Municipal corporation subcontractors.

Here, too, is a lot of confusion. The Federal Government is supposed to be composed of three (3) branches — (1) the actual Federal States of States (which have been mothballed since 1868), (2) the Territorial United States Government, and (3) the Municipal United States Government. All of these entities operate exclusively in the International Jurisdiction of the Sea, but there is another "Federal" Government, that which operates the International Jurisdiction of the Land owed to this country.

The adjective "Federal" actually refers to the "Federation of States" — the same States that are operated by the State Jural Assemblies. Our States formed their unincorporated Federation of States, The United States of America, on September 9, 1776. This is the Holding Company called a "Union" that operates the mutual International Land Jurisdiction functions of the States, so where more than one State is concerned,

Federal Marshals are hired by The United States of America to act as Peacekeeping Officers.

Notice that while actual elected County Sheriffs are called "Peacekeeping Officials", Federal Marshals are hired — not elected — and serve as "Peacekeeping Officers" employed by the Federation of States doing business as The United States of America.

As Americans have awakened and "returned" to the land and soil jurisdiction States of the Union, and our State Jural Assemblies have booted up, so has The United States of America been revived.

In 2015, we organized a new group of Federal Marshals, and in hopes of avoiding any more confusion between the sea-going "Federal Government" and the U.S. Marshals and the land-retaining Federation of States, we renamed the service: The Continental Marshals Service.

Almost immediately, more confusion arose.

The Continental Marshals Service is unincorporated, and these Federation of States Peacekeeping Officers outrank all U.S. Marshals and Agency Agents when standing on the land and soil of the States. Like the actual County Sheriffs, these men and women derive their authority from the Jural Assemblies of the States acting as a Federation of States and from the Public and Organic Law, not from any incorporated entity and not from any statutory law.

The Continental Marshals, like the old Federal Marshals, are Peacekeeping Officers of the Land and Soil, not Law Enforcement Officers of the Sea.

Another kind of Marshal is important to the proper functioning of the Land and Soil Government owed to the American States and People: the Provost Marshal.

This Office, too, has been grossly undermined and misconstrued by long abuse by corporate interests. Today, Provost Marshals are basically US Military Attorneys, operating as "liaison" officers and public affairs duty officers for the U.S. military. They come out of their hide-holes when a soldier goes off base and harms a local person, but largely ignore their actual and original duty as International Land Jurisdiction Peacekeeping Officers meant to act as Coordinators between the Federation of States and the U.S. Military.

Our American Government has always been supportive of the U.S. Military, but the two are not one-and-the-same. When in place on military bases located on our land and soil jurisdiction States, the U.S. Military is here as a guest, not as an Army of Occupation, as has too often been misconstrued and assumed by foreign interests.

There are occasions when the Provost Marshal, who is supposed to be acting as a Peacekeeping Officer for The United States of America, needs to run interference or coordinate activities between local State Officials, County Sheriffs, State Militia leaders and so on. The usurpation and mis-management of this position by foreign corporate military interests is a bone of contention to be resolved with the Territorial Government.

We must make it very clear that our States are the ultimate Employers of the U.S. Military and have never been anything else. The "States of States" that fought the Civil War on our soil were business entities operated by the States of America (Confederation), not The United States of America (Federation).

We had no dog in the fight and by no stretch of the imagination can our States or People be considered rebels, insurrectionists, enemies, or terrorists.

Finally, each State has a Marshal-at-Arms, who is responsible for the security of the State Jural Assembly, its records, its Officers, and its Membership during meetings, also for securing the Meeting Place prior to and immediately after meetings, and for Coordination of the County Militias with the State Militia. This is a very busy and important job. The Marshals-at-Arms for each State, like the leaders of the actual County and State Militias, are responsible for outreach and education of their counterparts in the U.S. Military, U.S. Marshals Service and LEO/law enforcement communities.

The Sheriffs are the key Peacekeeping Officials in each County and are among the first State Citizens elected to Public Office. As this brief overview shows, the actual People have been very poorly informed and even more poorly served regarding the differences between "peacekeeping" and "law enforcement" services.

As State Jural Assemblies have ceased to operate properly, more and more jobs have been taken over by incorporated foreign entities which have not been held to any solid standards of performance. In some cases, we have mob-linked corporations providing us with law enforcement services. It doesn't take rocket science to figure out the consequences of this situation.

The promulgation of private often foreign controlled "security services" corporations has left the situation not only confused, but in some cases, the absence or scarcity of the public peacekeeping forces has left whole sectors of our international jurisdiction unprotected or grossly undermanned. This has resulted in a very significant increase of crime.

Human trafficking, drug smuggling, mail and telephone fraud, counterfeiting, patent theft, identity theft, credit fraud, securities fraud, interstate bank fraud and numerous other crimes that are peculiar to international jurisdiction have skyrocketed because the International Land Jurisdiction turf of the old Federal Marshals has been vacated and neglected. U.S. Marshals have been underfunded and misdirected and understaffed so that they have not covered –or been able to cover — the international land jurisdiction as well as their own responsibilities.

This may be a matter of misplaced oversight, or another example of "accidentally on purpose" neglect being practiced by criminal elements that have had a much freer hand to operate since the old Federal Marshals program was phased out.

With the State Jural Assemblies coming back online and being brought up to speed, we can once again enforce the Public and Organic Law that the American States and People are owed. With your help, as observers and researchers, and with your participation in the State Jural Assemblies and Militias, we can enforce the actual Public Law, fill the gaps by hiring new Continental Marshals to cover our International Land Jurisdiction, and greatly improve the security and peace of our local communities.

For All the Jural Assemblies – 15

Coroners

The Office of County Coroner, like the Office of County Sheriff, has to be filled and is, in fact, one of the Primary Offices of the American Government. Why?

The Coroner is the only Public Official who can remove a sitting Governor from office. Strange, but true.

The logic of this is too convoluted and ancient to go into, but there is a long history confirming that of all the Public Offices, the Office of the Coroner is "the office of greatest trust".

This has in part to do with certification of whether or not people are "alive" or "dead", and this is why when Britain and the Pope colluded to defraud our Government in Breach of Trust, they conscripted and licensed all our doctors and nurses as "Uniformed Officers" (Territorial Federal Code Title 37).

They then imposed upon the medical professionals with coercive force to participate in the infamous Dead Baby Scheme. Our doctors are forced to "certify" the birth and death of "Human Persons"– what we call "afterbirths" —and to seize upon the expelled tissues and DNA, which the collaborators in the for-hire "government" register as "unclaimed" chattel property. In this way, the perpetrators lay a secretive and unconscionable commercial claim to our unique DNA.

We are somewhat hampered in our efforts to put an end to these schemes and an end to these absurd and abusive commercial claim activities by the simple fact that all the doctors and nurses are being coerced to participate in this fraud under pain of losing their licenses and ability to earn a living.

It becomes a "chicken and egg" proposition — in order to fully function, the actual land and soil jurisdiction government requires a Coroner, who must be a competently trained medical professional, but almost all the medical professionals have been trapped into accepting a license and subjecting themselves to the British Territorial United States Government instead of retaining their private status and functioning as State Nationals.

Thus, they wind up having to support a system they hate and which enslaves them, and most do not know that they have a choice and aren't actually required to have a license. All the "licensing" is being done by foreign, for-profit corporations and applies only to their subcontractors — contractors they have to actually hire or induct formally into the military before they can demand any licensing.

Once again, we are being entrapped by our own ignorance and willingness to "go along to get along". The doctors and nurses and dentists are actually being hoodwinked into complying with "laws" that do not and cannot apply to them, and they tie the proverbial noose around their own necks by applying for and accepting a license in the first place.

The situation is irritating on all sides, but there are ways to get around the need for a competent Coroner. Retired Medical Doctors and Nurses who no longer use their license can return it and serve as County Coroners. Men and women trained as Physician's Assistants in the course of their military training who, for whatever reasons, did not choose to make use of that training in private life can serve as Coroners.

Realistically, all that is needed is someone who has reasonable training and experience to be able to certify that a man is dead and to give an educated opinion of the cause of death. At first, anyway, the actual County Coroner serves only cases involving members of the State Jural Assembly (State Citizens) and those who have recorded their State National political status with the State Jural Assembly Recorder.

This makes for light duty at the present time, but as more Americans wake up and "return home" to the land and soil jurisdiction of their birth, the workload for the actual County Coroners will increase.

As well as recording deaths, County Coroners have an even more important function from the standpoint of the Jural Assembly: recording births. As new babies are born into the families of State Jural Assembly members and also into the families of State Nationals, the event and the details need to be recorded on the land and soil jurisdiction of the actual States.

The actual County Coroner's Office certifies both births and deaths and has them recorded by the State Jural Assembly Recorder's Office prior to serving Notice to the Territorial Government by providing a copy of the public record.

In all these functions, the State Jural Assembly and its members are the actual "Public" and the for-hire Territorial "State of State" corporations are "private" enterprises under contract to provide services to us— it is, in fact, the exact opposite from what most people assume.

Most people assume that the for-hire corporations are the actual government, because they have been unknowingly conscripted into the foreign jurisdiction of these corporations, and subjected to their private "law", so that these corporations which are merely providing "governmental services" appear to be the only actual government and their "statutory law" appears to be the only form of law.

However, once your State Jural Assembly rears its head and its Members are properly documented, the actual Public and Organic Law come back into view and into play and the cobwebs and deceits fade away.

For All The Jural Assemblies – 16

Notaries

The actual Office of the Public Notary is very important and very powerful. Our Notaries carry more power and hold a higher office than their corporate State of State Chief Justices. The problem has been that we haven't been able to access our Public Notaries and have had to rely on (from our perspective) "Notary Publics" instead, because our State Jural Assemblies haven't been operating properly and haven't been electing and confirming our State Public Notaries.

This is a good place to explain "the Federal Mirror".

Our Public is their Private, and vice-versa, from our respective viewpoints. This is because they are operating two foreign governments — one Territorial, one Municipal — on our shores.

From their perspective, the Federal Constitutions are "the Law of the Land", but from our perspective, these same documents are "the Law of the Sea". Why? Because from their perspective, these agreements dictate how they operate when they "come ashore" and interact with the Land Jurisdiction, but from our perspective, these agreements dictate how our employees, who are all operating exclusively in the Sea Jurisdiction, are supposed to operate with respect to us.

Thus, when you read "Federal Code" and "Federal Statutes", and the "State of State Codes" and "State of State Statutes" of their franchises, you will find references to foreigners. and "nonresident aliens". From their perspective as foreign governments, that's you. You are "nonresident" and "alien" with respect to them and their watery Territorial domain — that is, you are not a Territorial or Municipal Citizen.

And the same thing is true in reverse. Federal employees are acting in capacities and in a jurisdiction that is literally "foreign" and "alien" with respect to us.

The States have only one kind of "citizenship" — State Citizenship — but the Federales can have Dual Citizenship.

Dual Citizenship means a single man has obligations, and rights and duties, conferred by two or more governments.

Originally, employees of the Territorial and Municipal United States governments were allowed to claim (from the perspective of those governments) Dual Citizenship, because they couldn't get Americans to work for them otherwise. Thus Americans working for the Federal Government could furlough, but retain their

American State Citizenship while working as "U.S. Citizens".

Both Military and Civilian Federal Employees have always been obliged to adopt "U.S. Citizenship" while in the employment of the Federal Government, but such "citizenship" is supposed to be of a "transitory" nature that is supposed to terminate automatically upon them leaving such employment, retiring from such employment, or dying. That is, their "reversion" to State National political status is supposed to be automatic.

Unfortunately, like many other self-interested policies perpetuated by corporations in the business of providing governmental services, this recordkeeping was "accidentally-on-purpose" neglected and former Federal Employees have been routinely "presumed" to "voluntarily" stay in the status of U.S. Citizens until and unless their former Federal Employers are notified otherwise.

Many men and women who have been grateful to leave the military behind and many former Federal Civilian Service employees who have been grateful to retire, have been secretively "retained" and left on the record as "U.S. Citizens" — an unconscionable practice which has served to deny these loyal Americans the Natural and Unalienable Rights and constitutional guarantees they are heir to.

[It also means that people leaving Federal Employment have to look to this detail for themselves and State Jural Assemblies must make reasonable efforts to make sure that their Members and State Nationals recording their permanent domiciles have properly Notified all prior Federal Employers of their return home to their natural birthright political status.]

Today, Federales including (primarily Democratic) Congress Members use these Dual Citizenship provisions to claim citizenship in foreign countries like Israel or Japan and have no relationship at all with the actual American States they are claiming to "represent". That makes it easier for them to sell the actual States and People down the drain with no consequences for themselves and creates an intrinsic undeclared conflict of interest.

As a result of all this, when we think of something as "public" as in "Public Notary" we are thinking of our Public Notaries, which are Public Officials, but when they think of "Public Notary" they are thinking of their "Public Notaries", which are private corporate officers.

From our perspective, their "Public Notaries" are like their "Sheriffs" —working in a totally different jurisdiction and in separate, private corporate for-hire positions, even while performing a "Public" function.

Their private corporate "Public Notaries" like

their "Sheriffs" can put on a different hat and serve the Public Law if they want to, but as private vendors they can also refuse to serve in a "public capacity".

Our land and soil jurisdiction Public Notaries are "confirmed" in Office as elected Public Officials. They use stamps and red ink.

Their sea jurisdiction "Public Notaries" are "commissioned" as "Officers" of their private State of State corporations. They use seals and blue ink.

Again, we see the difference between an "Official" and an "Officer".

While our State Jural Assembly Recorders keep and transfer records as appropriate for Jural Assembly Members and State Nationals, and also officially record the actions taken by the State Jural Assembly itself, our Public Notaries process and witness and transfer the Public Records of the County, the State, and the People.

Our Public Notaries are members of our County and State Courts and hold a position of trust similar to that of a State Justice or County Justice of the Peace. Properly overseen Due Process Proceedings subject to Declaratory Judgment by an elected Public Notary have the full force and effect of the Public Law and cannot be reviewed or overturned by any private agency or "State of State" Court.

Each actual Public Notary elected should be rigorously trained in Due Process Proceedings and supplied with a red ink Public Notary Stamp saying simply:

"Ohio Notary" – for example, some distinctive design or logo, and the term of their Office like this: "In Office: 1 September 2016 to 30 November 2019."

Jural Assemblies are free to accept and adopt unique logos for their use and should formally do so while in session and should record images of the logos they are using and attach a small "c" in a circle copyright notice to the artwork or designs their Recorders and Notaries are using to stamp paperwork.

The often thankless work of a good elected Public Notary is an invaluable service to the State, the Counties, and the People. They provide a reliable and official Witness to the business transactions and records upon which we depend to secure our identities and control our assets and invoke the Public and Organic Law owed to our country.

For All The Jural Assemblies – 17

Clerks and Bondsmen

There are two Offices in our Public Courts that derive from the ancient Ecclesiastical Courts: Clerks were originally Clerics and Bondsmen were Bondsmen of Christ.

Clerks set the venue of court cases– that is, they determine where a case belongs, in which court and jurisdiction, and they assign it to a specific Judge, a Justice, or a Justice of the Peace to "shepherd" the proceedings.

So the first duty of a Court Clerk is to recognize the kind of action being pursued and the nature of the people or the persons pursuing it, and thereby, to correctly direct it to the appropriate jurisdiction and the appropriate court within that jurisdiction.

For many years now (since around 1965 in most places) Court Clerks have had no "People Courts" to refer people to. All the Public Courts we are owed were unlawfully converted into private courts serving only "Persons" when our often disloyal and often clueless employees incorporated the Territorial States of States and then the Counties, and began operating them as local franchises of federal corporations in exchange for federal kickbacks.

Now we have overcome the presumption and mistakes that led to this situation and are engaged in the process of setting up the Public Courts owed to the people of this country again. To start, we will only be serving the members of State Jural Assemblies– because we are the only "people" to serve.

Everyone else has been reduced to "personhood" via a process of adhesion contracts and non-disclosure and fraud.

Unfortunately, until they all wake up and explicitly change their "presumed" political status, and join the State Jural Assembly, they are outside our jurisdiction just as they are outside of ours.

Our Clerks have to turn away people who are coming to our courts seeking redress while still functioning as "foreign persons" on our shores.

This can be determined simply by asking if they are members of a State Jural Assembly? And by looking at the subject of the case.

Does it involve one of the People?

Does it involve things that occurred within the boundaries of our State or at the County level, inside our County?

Is it an issue that pertains to the land and soil and to actual, factual people and things?

That is our jurisdiction.

Or is it something intangible and theoretical, like two corporations arguing over patent rights? That is THEIR jurisdiction.

A good Court Clerk can determine the jurisdiction of a case from determining the capacity in which parties to a case are acting, the nature of the controversy and what it involves as subject matter.

Obviously, though a great many living people have valid issues that need to be addressed– so long as they continue to act as "persons" instead of choosing to act as people, we are powerless to assist.

If they continue to knowingly or unknowingly subject themselves to private incorporated courts –and be abused accordingly, there isn't much, if anything we can do.

JOHN O. KING vs. JOANN A.KING seeking a DIVORCE and voiding of their MARRIAGE LICENSE are two Municipal Corporations wanting to end a JOINT VENTURE ENTERPRISE and asking their parent corporation (the entity granting the license) and Silent Partner for permission to dissolve this business enterprise.

There isn't a living man or woman involved in that whole scenario.

So even though it impacts two people and

their children and everything they own, they can't be treated as people because they didn't act as people to begin with.

To get out of this situation they would have to petition the entity issuing the Marriage License and give Notice that they made a mistake.... and annul the "marriage" instead of seeking a DIVORCE.

A good Court Clerk operating a lawful Court as one of the People and a member of the State Jural Assembly can "observe the facts" though not offer "legal advice" since our lawful system is foreign to their legal system.

Court Clerks also maintain meticulous records of all the paperwork involved in a case, assigning numbers to case records and keeping track as more paperwork and evidence comes in and is added to the court record.

Land and soil jurisdiction Courts keep records. Sea jurisdiction Courts keep files.

Many Paralegals can readily fulfill the duties of Court Clerk once they are brought up to speed and understand that we are reopening Public Courts to serve the people (State Nationals) and People (State Citizens) of our State.

Bondsmen are the land counterparts to the Bailiffs in sea jurisdiction courts.

In early times the Ecclesiastical Courts had

Bondsmen serve to keep order in the court, but even more, to serve in the capacity of "brother's keeper". This is a role at the court level, to take charge of prisoners and ensure their safety and good conduct while in court. This role can also extend beyond the boundaries of the Court as Bondsmen may assist Sheriffs and other Public Law Officials in performance of their duties.

Just as the Clerks determine venue and keep the records, Bondsmen maintain the security of the actual courtroom and direct traffic within it. They may also seat people in the court gallery, help those who are physically injured or disabled, distribute educational information to members of the Jural Assembly, instruct people on how to post bonds –fees guaranteeing future performance of actions–that are retained and accounted for by the Court Clerk's Office, and act in similar capacities. A Bondsman may serve as a Witness to official paperwork and confirms the Bond Roster for each day the Court is in Session– he signs the list of Bonds set by the Court and confirms receipt of bonding fees together with the Court Clerk at the close of the Court's business each day. He secures and locks the safe containing the bond fees.

The Bondsmen typically make a public affirmation declaring that he will serve the People of the State in Good Faith and Honor, to protect the Court and the Public, and to assist in providing and securing peace and justice for all.

A similar simple Declaration (no Oaths, no "so help me God"– those are the for sea courts) applies to all Court Officials.

A written copy of this Declaration is kept in the Court Clerk's Office available for viewing along with the similar Declarations of the Justices and other officials.

The Bondsman in a court is meant to be a reassuring figure for those participating in or witnessing the proceedings, as well as a stalwart protector of everyone concerned, including those accused of crimes.

At first, there will be only a small number of the People functioning as people (State National) and People (State Citizens) and it will take time for them to close out transactions that were purposefully or mistakenly undertaken in the capacity of persons.

This affords the State Jural Assemblies the opportunity to get firmly established and work out the details and procedures and record-keeping before they are faced with an avalanche of caseloads.

It is to be hoped that when presented with the facts and the history many members of the Bar Associations will revoke their memberships and choose to serve the Public Courts and the people of their States as Counselors in Law and also to be hoped that many Judges and Magistrates will accept actual Public Office as Justices and Justices of the Peace.

The actual power of the Law is in the Public Law and in the Divine Law that underlies it.

The shameful and indeed criminal misapplication of statutory law to people unconscionably kidnapped in its jurisdiction as babies cannot be condoned and cannot be continued.

Each and every court case that is misaddressing living Americans in the NAME of such corporate franchises is evidence of crimes of personage and fraud against the Public Law and against our States and our People.

Confronted with these facts those running and administering these foreign corporate Courts/COURTS on our shores must come to terms with the crimes and injustices they have perpetuated against millions of innocent people, and the damage they have secretively done to this country for their own profit.

For All The Jural Assemblies – 18

Jurors and Citizenships

As explained before, the soil is defined as the top six inches of the land. The soil jurisdiction is our national jurisdiction, while the land under-lying it is our attached international land juris-diction. Because the two are inextricably com-bined, we speak of "the land and soil" of our States, and rarely have cause to look at the soil jurisdiction as a separate issue, but such it is.

All Americans start their lives as "state na-tionals", a political status known as "jus soli" or "man of the soil". We have no citizenship — that is, no obligation to serve any government. In-stead, what we acquire at birth is our national-ity. We are considered virginians, or ohioans or wisconsinites depending on where we are born.

At the level of soil jurisdiction our states are also written without any capital letters: virginia, ohio, wisconsin. These states are members of the original union of states known as The United States formed July 1, 1776, published and de-clared July 4, 1776.

As a practical matter, because soil is joined to land, we usually refer only to their "combined estate" of "land and soil" represented internationally by the States: Virginia, Ohio, Texas, et alia. And we refer to ourselves as Virginians, Ohioans, Texans, and so on.

These States thus offer and include four different possible political statuses:

(1) state nationals, (2) state citizens, (3) State Nationals, and (4) State Citizens.

If we wish to operate our states as nations, we drop back to our soil jurisdiction and operate as member states of The United States.

If we wish to operate our states as international entities, we operate our land jurisdiction States and operate as member States of The United States of America.

Both The United States and The United States of America are unincorporated entities. Together with their respective member states/States, they represent the "soil" and the "land" of this country.

It has been many years since the people of this country operated their soil jurisdiction states and The United States as "state citizens" and "one of the people", though there is no doubt that they have every right to do so. It is also rare for anyone to claim their original "jus soli" non-citizen capacity, but not totally unknown.

For our purposes at hand, we need to zero in on our States — Virginia, Ohio, Minnesota, et alia. These exist and operate in the International Jurisdiction of the Land.

We may operate as State Nationals or as State Citizens, both considered to be part of the "People" inhabiting the State.

A State National owes no obligation to serve the State Government. State Citizens accept the voluntary duty to serve their State Government.

The fundamental unelected voluntary Office underlying the authority of our States is that of Juror, a Member of the State Jural Assembly.

Just so we are clear — a State National and State Citizen may both claim to be "Virginians" or "Minnesotans", but one — the State National — has no official capacity and no particular duty to serve their State.

State Citizens, including the Jurors making up the State Jural Assembly, do owe a duty to the State Government according to the Office they have accepted or been elected to serve.

By joining the State Jural Assembly you are agreeing to serve as a Juror and act in the capacity of a State Citizen. This "Jury Duty" is the fundamental building block underlying the Public and Organic Law of this country.

Please note that thanks to identity theft and fraud practiced against us by our employees running the federal government, most of us have been mis-identified as Federal Citizens of one kind or another.

This necessitates recording our actual political status in rebuttal of these false claims and returning our Good Names — the Given Names our parents first gave us — to the "land and soil" of our home State and permanently domiciling our Names on the land and soil jurisdiction. It also necessitates us claiming all the various Territorial and Municipal franchise Names/ NAMES that have been associated with us and returning those to the land jurisdiction of our States and re-flagging and re-domiciling them, too.

Please be aware that our states and States are both outside and foreign to the Federal States of States, the Territorial States of States, and the Municipal STATES OF STATES —and also foreign to any form of "federal" citizenship attached to these states-of-states.

In addition to our possible citizenships if we choose to serve our state (The United States) and our State (The United States of America), there are three common "federal" citizenships that exist only in the international jurisdiction of the sea. These foreign citizenships apply only to federal employees, dependents, and foreign corporations created under federal auspices.

As you will see, Federal States of States are supposed to exist and operate under names like this: The State of Maine, The State of Florida,…. and these are supposed to be inhabited by Federal Civil Servants including United States Senators and Members of the House of Representatives, Federal Judges, and Federal Officers.

Their form of citizenship is described under Article 1, Section 3, Clause 3 as "United States Citizenship". This is a foreign citizenship with respect to us and to our States, one that exists in the International Jurisdiction of the Sea and which is designed to represent our States by delegating some of our State's powers to the Federal States of States.

Unfortunately, this system broke down in 1868.

Instead, we have employees of the British Territorial United States of States usurping upon the States and the Federal States of States, and substituting their foreign, British Territorial "States of States". These also have their own form of citizenship which applies to their employees, which is described under Article 1, Section 2, Clause 2 as "Citizens of the United States".

The Federal States of States are meant to serve our States, and the Territorial States of States are meant to serve the Federal States of States.

Finally, thanks to Article 1, Section 8, Clause 17, there is the Municipal Government, a plenary oligarchy run by members of (at this point) the Territorial United States "Congress" — and their employees have their form of citizenship, too — slavery.

The point is– all these "federal" forms of citizenship involving obligation to serve Federal "States of States" or Territorial "States of States" or Municipal "STATES OF STATES" — are foreign to us and foreign to our land jurisdiction States.

They and their citizenships have nothing to do with us except that they are supposed to be working for us and our States, exercising some of our Delegated Powers, and providing us with "Good Faith" and "Service" under the constitutional contracts that apply to the Federal, Territorial, and Municipal United States Governments.

As for us, and our State Jural Assemblies, this is where the pedal hits the metal in making all other aspects of government work and enforcing the Public and Organic Law of this country again.

If you want to end the madness and the uncontrolled avarice of undeclared foreign "federal" service organizations running rampant on our shores— reclaiming your actual birthright political status and choosing to serve your state/ State as a Jural Assembly Member are the first two steps.

The fundamental Office of Juror is "accepted" as a "duty" and is not elected.

Anyone born on the soil of one of the states and who foreswears all foreign allegiances (Act of Expatriation from Federal, Territorial, or Municipal status) can serve as a Juror in a State Jural Assembly.

Our States of the Union do not recognize any Dual Citizenship whatsoever, so if you are going to serve as a State Jural Assembly Member, that is, as a Juror, you must voluntarily give up any attachment to any foreign government — which includes the various citizenships of the federal entities operating as "states of states".

Resolving these issues and clarifying your actual political status and the capacity in which you are choosing to act is the purpose of all the paperwork that has to be done before you can lawfully serve as a Juror and Member of your State Jural Assembly.

So what does a qualified Juror do, once you have hopped through all the hoops and re-established your identity as an American standing on American soil?

Jurors form the Jury Pool for your State.

You may be called upon to hear court cases as a Trial Juror or to participate in bringing charges as a member of a Grand Jury.

As a State Jural Assembly Member your are also pre-qualified to function as a County Jural Assembly Member, and vice-versa, so you may be called upon to help fill the local jury pools as a Trial Juror or as a member of the County Grand Jury, too.

Our State Trial Jurors listen to the unique cases presented and decide the Law and the Facts. This is fundamentally different than the duties of "State of State" Juries, which cannot consider the Law or the Facts, but only the statutes, codes, and regulations that govern the various federal-based corporations, their franchises, and their employees.

State Jural Assemblies enforce the Public and Organic Law. They are enabled to address the Public Law and the Facts of individual cases, both.

State of State Jural Societies enforce Statutes (statutory "law"), Codes, and Regulations on their employees, dependents, and members.

Our State Grand Jury Jurors listen to allegations of crime against the Public and Organic Law and decide whether or not there is sufficient cause to present charges for prosecution. Their deliberations result in "indictments" being issued against foreign citizens (including federal citizens) or in "presentments" being issued against State Nationals or State Citizens.

The most important function beyond fair deliberation and enforcement of the Public and Organic Law that our State Jural Assemblies and Jurors perform is Jury Nullification.

Our State Jural Assembly Members acting as Jurors in actual Trials can throw out any law that they find repugnant to the Public Good or the Cause of Justice.

Our Jural Assembly Members can pass judgment on all acts of legislation affecting our States and People, including acts of any Federal Congress, any Territorial Congress, or any Municipal Congress that usurps upon our security or offers to disrespect our Natural and Unalienable Rights.

This process of lawful Jury Nullification is designed to prune over-reaching legislative activity on the part of our employees, who are only authorized to organize and regulate their own activities and duties in accord with their constitutional contracts.

Our State Courts are enabled to hear cross-jurisdictional cases involving private businesses and State Nationals and State Citizens versus federal, territorial, and municipal incorporated businesses and franchises.

The Wisconsin Court can hear cases like: "The People of Wisconsin vs. GENERAL ELECTRIC, INC." or "John Robert Fox vs. State of Idaho" and is able to hear and judge both the law and the facts, and throw out anything that offends the Jurors.

Nullification of a statutory State of State law or even an Act of any Federal, Territorial, or

Municipal Congress results in it being declared null and void.

It may take awhile for this to sink in and for "federal" and "state of state" employees to come to heel, but this is the actual power of the People being exercised as it is meant to be exercised.

As more of the people come home to the land and soil jurisdiction of their States and accept their duty to act in the capacity of Jurors and as State Citizens— one of the People referenced in the Constitutions—-the Public and Organic Law of the actual State and of the country as a whole, is enforced.

We can do away with such evil inanities as "Legalized Lying" — 18 USC 1001, Subsection A and B, and enforce the Public Law against such evils as "Legalized Infanticide" that our out-of-control public employees have proposed.

We can enforce our standards on them because they are our employees; their Acts and statutory law must conform to our Public and Organic Law or be overturned and remain unenforceable.

Thus when our State's Public Law declares that infanticide is premeditated murder and a capital crime, it avails the foreign corporations operating on our shores nothing to pretend that the Public Policies of their corporations prevail.

Our Sheriffs and Deputies overstand their for-hire Pinkerton Law Enforcement Officers. Our Jurors decide both the validity of the law — whatever kind of law it is — and the facts.

It is worth noting here that our Judicial Officials working for the State Jural Assemblies do not decide the law or the facts in any case. Our Judicial Officials act to ensure an even playing field where both the law and the facts of a case may be knowledgeably discussed and fully vetted by our Jurors.

The Judicial Officials are responsible for holding the operations of the Court to established and accepted standards of evidence — for example, recognizing inadmissible hearsay presented as evidence. As such, our Judicial Officials can verify records, administer court procedures, offer insight when asked for it, shepherd cases through Due Process requirements, and in all ways act to provide the foundation and decorum that allows justice to prevail.

It is the Jurors — the members of our jural assemblies — who decide all matters in our State and County Courts. The Justices pronounce their sentences, and the Recorder records them, and the Sheriffs enforce them.

The fundamental importance of the State Jural Assemblies and of the Jurors who make them possible cannot be overstated. By promoting and lawfully enforcing the Public and Organic Law of this country, these organizations protect Americans and American assets from the unrestricted predations and presumptions of foreign corporations and their employees.

The health and strength of the State Jural Assemblies is a direct measure of the health and strength of our country as a whole. There can be no greater duty set before any American than the duty to "come home" to the land and soil jurisdiction and join their State Jural Assembly.

For All The Jural Assemblies – 19

The Public and Organic Law

As stupefying as it is, the Public Law of this country has not been enforced in any organized and comprehensive fashion for at least fifty years. Instead, a semblance, or as they themselves put it — an "appearance of justice" —has been provided by private corporate "courts" operated by private "self-governing" jural societies.

These "jural societies" as opposed to "jural assemblies" operate in the international jurisdiction of the sea and administer its statutory law. They can only address "Persons"— that is, corporations and corporation employees, and they have no authority to address living people at all, much less one of the People who are their employers.

So how have they gotten away with usurping upon us and our government and commandeering millions of Americans into their foreign sea jurisdiction courts?

They have gotten away with addressing people as "persons" via a process of falsification of records called "registrations". These registration documents then provide the excuse for them to "presume" that we are "volunteering" to act as corporate franchisees, subject to whatever private, internal corporate "laws" they concoct and impose upon their franchises—- exactly like Burger King or Dairy Queen franchises.

This is, of course, a form of organized crime—fraud and enslavement resulting in peonage and racketeering, that is abhorrent to the Public Law of this country and most countries on Earth.

As more county and state jural assembly organizations converted (unlawfully) to operate as corporate franchises of the Territorial and/or Municipal United States in order to receive federal racketeering kickbacks, the enforcement of the Public and Organic Law, including the Constitutions, has been left to volunteers — like Sheriff Richard Mack — and officials entering vacated public offices via small electorate elections — like me.

The increasingly insane and lawless results of letting private foreign corporations run our government and provide self-interested courts "for" us, are abundantly clear and require a strong and organized push back.

This is that lawful push back.

First, you rebut their registrations and presumptions, and reclaim your original birthright political status as an American standing on the land and soil of your State of the Union. You do this first to protect yourself from their false claims of authority over you and your property assets, and secondarily to qualify yourself to act as a State Jural Assembly Member. See www.annavonreitz.com, Article 928.

Next, you join your State Jural Assembly and organize it and grow it. See www.national-assembly.net, email contentmanager1@yahoo.com.

The State Jural Assemblies are the instruments we need to enforce the Public and Organic Law, which stands above all private, corporate forms of "law".

What this means in practical terms is that when they pass a private corporate law requiring doctors to murder babies on demand, we have the ability to enforce the public law that defines infanticide as murder and the promotion of murder as insurrection against the Public Law.

It also means that when one of their for-hire "Law Enforcement Officers" attempts to arrest or detain us while in the peaceful pursuit of our private business, we are empowered to invoke The Bill of Rights and Article IV of the Federal Constitution — and make it stick. On the spot.

We can also outlaw their registration practices on our shores and force the dismantling of their entire crime machine on our soil, so that new generations of Americans are not faced with the arduous process of reclaiming what should never have been lost.

If you are tired of letting immoral monsters pillage and plunder and harass and steal from honest people under color of law, its time to put the corporations out of their misery and put the people back in control.

Now that we finally know what we are up against, we know how to reply to it.

We know how to lawfully declare our political status and evidence it. We know how to implement our self-government in each State via populating and organizing our State Jural Assemblies, electing our Public Officials, and enforcing the Public and Organic Law this country is owed.

For All The Jural Assemblies – 20

Jurisdiction of People

It is of paramount importance for everyone involved in the State Jural Assemblies to understand the basics of jurisdiction. A jurisdiction is "invoked" or "claimed" as a result of the (1) subject matter and (2) capacity of the parties involved in a dispute.

A squabble over access to sea lanes between two naval vessels is obviously an admiralty issue, while a controversy over cow pasturage between two unincorporated farms in New Jersey is obviously a soil jurisdiction issue.

There are three basic jurisdictions possible — air, land, and sea, and three basic capacities, unincorporated, corporate, and incorporated, in which we may function, so a total of nine (9) different basic combinations.

In addition to this, there are two sub-sections to each of the basic jurisdictions and different kinds of law attached to each.

The Air Jurisdiction is divided into ecclesiastical (Pope) and municipal law (Pontiff). The Sea Jurisdiction (British Monarch/Britannic Majesty) is divided into maritime (aka "civil law" or "commercial law") and admiralty (martial law). The Land is divided into public and private law, or as they are more popularly known, common and statutory law.

Fortunately for you, you only need to be able to pinpoint and manage the two jurisdictions that you are responsible for (soil and land) and be able to direct your employees regarding how you want the rest of the business of your country handled (maritime and admiralty and municipal affairs).

Because our Forefathers established a "Secular State" and "separation between church and state" and "freedom of religion", the Jurisdiction of the Air is limited to Municipal Jurisdiction, which was confined to the ten miles square of the District of Columbia —and never intended to usurp beyond the Municipality of Washington, DC — though it has.

The three original Constitution(s) — Federal (1787), Territorial (1789) and Municipal (1790) established a National Will with regard to the administration of the Sea and Air Jurisdictions by our employees.

Please note that though the Constitutions provided them — our employees — with structures, corporate offices, rules, and service contracts, all of the functions of the resulting "Federal Government" are foreign to the land and soil jurisdiction that you and your State Jural

Assemblies are heir to.

Please also note from the nomenclature, that the Parties to the Constitutions establishing them — We, the People — are members of the State Jural Assemblies. Your State Jural Assemblies are responsible for enforcing the contracts thus established.

You are the Guardians of the Peace and the Enforcers of the Constitutions. Nobody else can do it and without your firm guidance, your employees —left to their own devices for 150 years— are in La-La Land.

The jurisdiction that is natural to living people is that of the national soil (people, counties, The United States) and international land (People, State, The United States of America). This is the realm of the State Jural Assemblies.

Because soil and land are attached to each other, qualification in the State Jural Assembly also qualifies you as part of your county jural assembly and vice versa, so that both the land and the soil jurisdictions are "populated" when you qualify as a Juror and join. That is, you are able and qualified to serve either the soil jurisdiction or the land jurisdiction, depending on which hat you put on and which court you serve.

Please note, especially, that your "State" and "County" Courts exist in a totally different jurisdiction than the "State of State" Courts and their corporate franchises operating "as" County

Courts.

You are operating on the "land and soil" of your State, addressing the issues that impact the living American people and their assets. You are invoking and enforcing the Public Law, including the Constitutions.

"They", the U.S. Citizens, are operating in the foreign international jurisdiction of the sea as part of an incorporated Territorial State of State franchise or in the foreign global jurisdiction of the air as an incorporated Municipal STATE OF STATE franchise. They are addressing the affairs and assets of legal fiction "Persons". They are enforcing the private law of their corporations on their employees and shareholders and franchises.

Do not make the mistake of thinking that their courts are your courts. They aren't. These foreign courts are for the most part occupying courthouses that you bought and paid for, but they are like a baseball team occupying a public ball field.

Your courts have a pre-eminent right to use these facilities, and part of what remains to be resolved is for your State Jural Assembly — once it is fully populated and organized and you have qualified your Electors (not "Voters") and you have held your elections to fill your Offices — is to inform the State of State Governor that you are in full operation and wish to occupy your own State Buildings, including Courthouses, again.

At first, there may be friction against this idea, but the ultimately, the State of State Courts and their personnel have no choice but to shift over and let you make use of the Public Facilities. This is because you are running the actual Public Courts.

It is also a necessity, because without a State, they have no State of State. Even if their "State of State" corporation is organized under the auspices of a foreign country, as they currently are, they cannot define themselves "of" a non-existent State.

So they need you to maintain the land and soil jurisdiction States as much as you need them to honor and obey the provisions of the Constitutions that authorize their existence.

As you form up your State and County Courts and more people "return" to their birthright political status as Americans and relinquish (gladly for the most part) any presumed "U.S. Citizenship", the Courts you operate are again enabled to invoke jurisdiction over soil and land issues and to enforce the Public Law, including the provisions of the Constitutions and their guarantees owed to the people of this country.

With your courts operating and invoking jurisdiction, a situation like the nightmare that the Bundy family went through over "grazing rights" cannot occur. Why? Because the BLM is only a care-taker of the soil and land resources of the Western States, and the Bundys — assuming that they declare their birthright political status — are "recognizable" as the actual Landlords that the BLM works for.

The nightmare of the Foreclosure Mills goes away, too, because the foreign Territorial Courts and Municipal COURTS no longer have any trust property to administer. The land trusts dissolve upon the arrival of the people back home on the land and soil of their States and all their "personal" trusts held under false presumptions are also converted and re-flagged as "persons" belonging to Americans, not "U.S. Citizens" or "Citizens of the United States".

The jurisdiction of the people/People on the land and soil of their States is absolute, unincorporated, and sovereign. The unincorporated County and State Court Juries established by your unincorporated County and State Jural Assemblies have the ability to nullify any corporate statute, rule, or regulation, any "Federal Code" and can keep these foreign statutes and codes from being applied to any of the people of this country.

It is true that both the Territorial and Municipal government service providers are under contract to also provide protection to our "persons" and "property". That being so, many Americans will be left shaking their heads in view of abuses they have suffered in Territorial and Municipal Courts, where they have been addressed as "persons" belonging to the foreign Territorial and Municipal Corporations.

A key understanding is that "U.S. Citizens" are not owed the protections of the Constitutions nor the protections of the Public Law. While acting "as" and allowing themselves to be characterized as "U.S. Citizens" –Americans who are otherwise eligible to be recognized as Americans, are instead being classified as foreigners — as Territorial or Municipal United States Citizens. They are not acting in the capacity of State Nationals or State Citizens who are owed the protections of the Constitutions and who occupy the land and soil jurisdiction of this country. They are instead being deliberately misidentified as Territorial or Municipal United States citizens.

The Territorial and Municipal service providers only recognize their duty to protect the persons and property of the people —pay attention to the word: "people"—of this country, that is, those who occupy the land and soil jurisdiction, and do not honor any similar obligation to their own officers and employees and franchisees.

Thus, when you expatriate from any form of Federal Citizenship, and embrace your birthright citizenship as a State Citizen and member of your State Jural Assembly, the Public and Organic Law comes back into force, and the Territorial "State of State" and Municipal "STATE OF

STATE" courts can no longer presume anything about you, your assets, your property, or your persons. They have to backwater and treat you as one of the People of this country.

For All The Jural Assemblies – 21

Capacity of the People

While the subject matter of a case will often immediately determine the correct jurisdiction and court to hear it, the issue of "capacity in which the Parties act" is by no means as clear-cut, and requires due diligence.

Consider the sentence: "Marc is one of the people who built the Cross River Bridge." "Marc" is obviously a man who helped build a bridge and he did so in an unincorporated capacity, because the word "people" was used.

If we said, "Marc is one of the persons who built the Cross River Bridge." we would have an entirely different flavor and meaning. This would imply that "Marc" is the name of a corporation or business of some kind that was involved in building the bridge.

It's the same name, Marc, but different capacities are indicated. This applies all across the board:

Marc Allen Jones is a member of our football team. [Unincorporated Capacity]

Marc Allen Jones is American. [Corporate

Capacity — International Trade — International Land Jurisdiction]

Marc Allen Jones, Inc. provides tax accounting services. [Incorporated Capacity — International Commerce – International Jurisdiction of the Sea]

We, too, can choose to act in the capacity of one of the people (our national soil jurisdiction) or one of the People (our international land jurisdiction) or as a Person — (international sea jurisdiction or municipal jurisdiction).

When we act as one of the People standing on our international land jurisdiction, we use a Trade Name, like "John Michael Downing". We use the same "style" of Proper Name while operating as a "United States Person" in the international jurisdiction of the sea.

It's the same name, but two different jurisdictions, two different capacities.

The entire Great Fraud which has been worked against us and our country has hinged on that fact and that our employees are accidentally-on-purpose misunderstanding the capacity in which we are acting.

"John Michael Downing", one of the People of Minnesota, standing peacefully as a State Citizen on the international land jurisdiction of Minnesota, is owed all the guarantees of the Constitutions and international treaties he is heir to. If he goes to sea (enters international sea jurisdiction) the British Monarch owes him protection. If he enters municipal jurisdiction, the Pope owes him protection.

"John Michael Downing", a "U.S. Citizen", acting in the capacity of a Person adrift on the international jurisdiction of the sea without a declared permanent domicile, has no guarantees, no treaties, and is presumed to be a Ward of the Territorial State of Minnesota or the Municipal STATE OF MINNESOTA. He has no constitutional guarantees or protections at all.

Those intent upon plundering and pillaging us have, of course, chosen to interpret the capacity in which we are acting to suit themselves and their purposes. They have been eager to mis-characterize us as "U.S. Citizens" living in Territorial "States of States" or Municipal STATES OF STATES instead of as Americans living in actual States of the Union—– and to abuse us accordingly.

When you knowledgeably take exception to this self-interested presumption and rebut it with pre-established evidence and join your State Jural Assembly, these foreign British Territorial and Municipal Courts are in a bind to excuse their predatory actions against their actual Employers and Hosts.

The shameful and criminal nature of their activities becomes apparent — but it only becomes apparent when you educate yourselves and formally declare your identity and capacity as a State Citizen, one of the People of your State, and of The United States of America.

Many Americans are fond of spouting off about "We, the People...." but they fail to recognize the jurisdiction and capacity that the "People" are operating in. There have been many arguments about the use of a capital "P" on the word "People" –but it is actually very simple.

One of the oddities of international jurisdiction, both land and sea, is that it is populated entirely by legal fiction entities — businesses, corporations, and the officers and offices of such businesses and corporations.

So, when the people of this country occupy their international land jurisdiction, and inhabit their States of the Union, they act in the capacity of Jurors or occupy other Offices of their State and as a group, act as the People of their States and as The People of The United States of America —- a lawful unincorporated Federation of their States.

The State itself is a Corporate entity — but it is unincorporated. We see this concept whenever we encounter a small independent business — "Jake's Dog Wash", for example, is "corporate" in that it is a legal fiction with a Proper Name, but it is not "incorporated" — i.e., it did not ask any other corporation to adopt it or give it privileges and it doesn't function under a charter granted by any other corporation.

Our own Given Names are naturally in the same status as our States— and operate in the same Corporate, but unincorporated capacity as our States of the Union and Jake's Dog Wash.

Unfortunately, the same style of Proper Name can be applied to Persons operating in the international jurisdiction of the sea as incorporated franchises of foreign Territorial and Municipal corporations, such as the British Territorial "State of Minnesota" or the Roman (Catholic) Municipal "STATE OF MINNESOTA".

And it is up to you to declare and provide evidence of the capacity in which you are choosing to act.

Our Forefathers sought to cut through this conundrum and avoid the possible attendant abuses of our people by the simple device of allowing us no other citizenship apart from State Citizenship. We either is or we ain't.

Once you become a Juror and Member of the your State Jural Assembly you are operating as a State Citizen and by definition no longer operating in any capacity as a "U.S. Citizen", voluntary or otherwise. This is because the States do not allow Dual Citizenship, and this stands as a safeguard for you against usurpation, false claims in commerce, and other evils that can otherwise be "presumed" against you by their foreign corporate tribunals.

You can operate as a State National or as a State Citizen, but you cannot at the same time operate as a U.S. Citizen or Citizen of the United States. The terms are mutually exclusive for our purposes.

Understandably, those who have benefited by mis-characterizing us and being able to abuse us by presuming that we are "voluntarily" acting in the capacity of "U.S. Citizens" are loathe to give up their pretenses and eager to obstruct our progress.

Our runaway Employees do not want to submit to the yoke of their Employers and do not want to respect and fulfill the binding treaties and constitutional service contracts that they have with our States of the Union. The tail has been wagging the dog for a long time and they want to continue spending our money and hypothecating debt against our assets "for" us.

Many Americans and other people around the world have complained that "the world is upside down", that those we employ to protect us are abusing us instead, that our courts provide anything but justice, that our medical care has been commandeered by Big Pharma, that our churches have become incorporated businesses more concerned with managing their investments than teaching any moral precepts.

You are not imagining things. The world is upside down. It is upside down because the employees are running the employers ragged. So it is up to you to assert your natural birthright capacity and political status, to accept your responsibilities as an American —- not as a "U.S. Citizen" —- and to set things to right in this country.

Nobody can object to this, as nobody has standing to object. Nobody can accuse you of being in "insurrection" nor "rebellion" once you firmly and clearly and knowledgeably declare your political status and the capacity in which you are acting.

In fact, it is our "federal employees" —both Territorial and Municipal—- who have flirted with insurrection and trespassed against the people of this country.

It is now your role and responsibility to act in the capacity of State Jural Assembly Members — as Jurors and as other Officers of the State and County Courts that the people of this country are owed, to put an end to any false and self-interested claims that we have "abandoned" our country, and act to enforce the Public and Organic Law.

For All The Jural Assemblies – 22

Overcoming Indoctrination

There is a force of indoctrination, which feels like a force of gravity, telling us that we don't have to do anything. Obviously, we can all just sit on our rumps and be served all the government services we could ever ask for—and more than we'd wish for or imagine in most cases.

That's what those who are in the business of providing all those government services want us to do: just keep ordering up more and more government services, more programs for the indigent, more welfare, more medical services, more "entitlements", more police, more military actions, more spy programs, more, more, more!

That's how they make their money, and for the sake of their profits, no thought of self-governance can be allowed to enter your heads.

Just be lazy, Joe. Go back to sleep. Leave it all to us–whoever we are. It will all be fine as long as you pay your taxes.

And we must admit, doing nothing is so seductive. It's so easy. Just drift along and let the servants be your masters. Don't check the price tag. Don't think too much.

Many of the State Jural Assemblies are aghast.

Their members and leaders are saying — "Wha-a-at? We are supposed to know and do all this? Why isn't this being taken care of for us? We are supposed to run our own State courts? Have our own State legislature meeting regularly?"

Yes.

This is what "self-governance" means. This is the way the American Government is supposed to work.

Many people got involved in this thinking that this would be a way to register their discontent with the government services providers—- which it is, but they weren't counting on the prospect of having to provide a parallel system of self-governance to operate the land and soil jurisdiction of this country. They somehow thought that if they complained enough, someone else would step forward and do it all for them, but nobody can.

There's a good deal of confusion about that reality also.

The land and soil jurisdictions of this country are yours. They belong to you. Your State belongs to you. Your Federal State of State, waiting for "reconstruction" since 1868, belongs to you. And nobody else can operate them or reconstruct them for you. Nobody in the world.

It's like that moment when a pregnant woman realizes, "This is it..." –and there is nobody else in the world who can give birth to that child.

Or the old hymn: "You gotta walk that lonesome valley, you gotta walk it by yourself, no, nobody else can walk it for you, you gotta walk it by yourself....."

Nobody can do it for you. Even if they wanted to, they can't.

It's up to Americans who claim their birthright political status, organized as lawful State Jural Assemblies, to enforce the Public and Organic Law of this country, including the Constitution(s).

It's up to us to provide ourselves with our own State and County Courts to serve the people — that is, those who are operating in their birthright capacity and occupying the land and soil jurisdiction of this country.

It's up to us to convene our own State Legislatures on a regular basis.

It's up to us to choose Deputies to send to our own Continental Congress and take care of land and soil jurisdiction business that has been hanging fire for decades.

And no, nobody can do it for us.

But, but, but......how, people wonder.....? We don't have a fat budget to provide these services for ourselves. All our money is going to foreign service providers so they can provide services to all the "Persons". We don't know how to run a court for people. We don't know how.... We do it the same way our Forefathers did. We hike up our skirts. We educate ourselves. We act and operate upon principles of Good Faith and Good Will. We volunteer. We get organized. We do our duty. We uphold the Public and Organic Law. We seize hold of the rights and freedoms that the people — notice that word: people, not persons — of this country are heir to.

In order to accomplish this for ourselves and our children and for the good of the entire world, we have to do the work. We have to revive the Public and Organic Law. We have to declare our birthright political status. At least some of us have to undertake the sacrifices and duties of State Citizens.

For All The Jural Assemblies – 23

Prior and Concurrent Assemblies

There is a great deal of confusion abounding about the subject of Prior Assemblies and Concurrent Assemblies.

Our actual American Government on the land and soil of this country has never ceased functioning. Part of our lawful government has been moth-balled at the level of the Federal States of States since 1860, but the States which hold the actual power of contract have continued to function throughout.

Likewise, false claims in commerce have been addressed to us and to our States and have been rebutted each time. Nothing that has happened since 1860 has gone forward without rebuttal of false claims against us and against our States.

Read that as — the British Tories and the Papal Legates have been trying to undermine our position as the lawful government of this country for a long, long time, and have never been able to succeed because of stubborn resistance and knowledgeable rebuttal of their claims.

This most recent round has been especially hard-fought. The bankers advanced many arguments in favor of their attempt to "inherit" our land jurisdiction as "abandoned property" left in the care of incompetent bankrupt secondaries (the bankrupt foreign Territorial and Municipal Corporations claiming to be our "caretakers" and "representatives").

Bankrupt and incompetent, they may be; but our States are not bankrupt and not incompetent, so the appropriate counter-claims have been made and the rebuttals to their offers have been published and we are in position to reclaim and restore and retain our rightful government.

Doing this work has required lawful inheritors of the States to step forward —and a lot of paperwork. These men have proven the provenance of ancestors "grandfathered in" prior to the American Civil War and meet all the other qualifications of Jurors in their State Jural Assemblies and have stood as place-keepers pending the calling of the State Jural Assemblies.

This is not a claim of "ownership" in the sense that Joe Adams owns Florida. This is a claim in behalf of all the qualified Jurors like Joe Adams who live in Florida and who claim their birthright political status as Floridians. The land assets and silver money and everything else of actual value belongs to Floridians, but the People have to stand up and claim it. This, in turn, requires withdrawing from any "presumed" obligation to act as "US Citizens" and Expatriating from any allegiance or obligation to the Territorial or Municipal United States.

Why? Because our Forefathers aimed to avoid exactly the kind of meddling that has occurred here by making sure that none of our actual States allow any form of Dual Citizenship.

The entities called "States of States" involved in administering the Federal Government and subjecting "United States Citizens" and "Citizens of the United States" all allow Dual Citizenship, but our States do not. Our actual States allow no conflicts of interest and no inclusion of split loyalties to foreign powers.

That again, is why Americans must stand as Americans and must Expatriate.

When we "return" to the land and soil of our States (we never actually left; FDR just gratuitously claimed that we did) and join our State Jural Assembly, we naturally become jurors of the soil jurisdiction and citizens of The United States at the same time that we become Jurors and Citizens of The United States of America.

Note the capital "T" —- The United States (soil) and The United States of America (land).

Our disloyal British Territorial employees have tried to "misunderstand" these facts and reinterpret this to mean that we are claiming to be

Citizens of the United States, (Article 1, Section 2, Clause 2) instead. This semantic deceit based on deceptively similar names — "citizens of The United States" versus "Citizens of the United States" has allowed them to presume upon us and our assets as if we were subjects of the Queen.

By refuting this on the Public Record and re-butting their presumptions we re-establish our identity as Americans and re-establish our property rights and interests, including the guarantees of the Constitutions we are owed.

By serving our States of the Union as State Jural Assembly members we breathe life back into our government "of the people, by the people, and for the people" — which is by definition not a government "of the persons, by the persons and for the persons" subject to the Queen or the Pope.

We honor the efforts of all those who have similarly gone before us and rebutted the false claims made against us, our States, and our countrymen by these foreign powers, both the British Monarchs and the Popes, whose governments owe us Good Faith Service under contract.

At this time, a certain amount of chaos persists as Americans wake up to the clear and present danger of the National Identity Theft being attempted and seek to get their State Jural Assemblies organized.

It is not uncommon for there to be more than one State Jural Assembly in operation in the same state at the same time. This is not any big reason for concern and certainly not a source of competition. All the local groups naturally coalesce into a single State Jural Assembly.

What is more important is that the Assemblies and their members grasp the urgent necessity that compels them to get organized and that we all do our duty to educate others and apply more or less uniform standards.

There are some groups out there on the fringes who claim, for example, that old court cases like Marbury vs. Madison protect us from the fraud being perpetuated upon us and that we needn't bother to reply to nor bother to rebut the false claims of our adversaries.

They don't get the point.

Our adversaries are not arguing against Marbury vs. Madison. They are arguing that you "voluntarily" gave up your birthright American Citizenship and accepted "Federal Citizenship" instead, and therefore, you are no longer protected by the constitutional agreements nor any of the case law such as Marbury vs. Madison.

According to them, it simply doesn't apply to you, and this is also the reason that U.S. District Court Judges have been known to hold people in contempt for advancing constitutional arguments in their courts.

We have to be qualified American State Nationals and American State Citizens —-and be claiming our status as such — or the Constitutional guarantees don't apply to us. Since we have all been left in the dark and not grasped the falsehoods being "presumed' upon us, we have been at a loss as to how to reply or what to reply to.

After all, their primary evidence against us and against our claim to be an American State National is the issuance of a Territorial or Municipal "Birth Certificate" that was purloined while we were still babes in our cradles, and it is upon the basis of this "unconscionable" contract —- literally a contract we are unconscious of — that they are prosecuting us in their foreign courts and under false legal presumptions.

How can we knowledgeably rebut evidence that is not presented to us in court and which results from a purported "private contract" that we know nothing about? How can we correctly rebut false presumptions if we don't know what the presumptions are? It's impossible.

This is why so many millions of Americans have been led like lambs to slaughter in these foreign Federal District Courts and "State of State"Courts.

The fundamental issue is never addressed, so all claims to be owed your "constitutional guarantees" fall on deaf ears.

If you are an American standing on American soil, what are you doing in a Federal District Court answering to the name of a British Territorial Citizen? Or worse, a Municipal CITIZEN? And why are you claiming to have any "constitutional rights" or guarantees, when it is plain as day that neither British Territorial nor Municipal CITIZENS have any such rights or guarantees?

Those who think that they can wave Marbury vs. Madison at these British Bounders or the acolytes of the Holy Roman Empire and get a free pass and who argue that they don't need to take any public action to rebut these false claims need to think again.

If you want to be protected instead of attacked and want the actions of your State Jural Assemblies to be internationally recognized and respected, then you must insist that your Members make public recorded Declaration of their permanent Expatriation from any presumed Federal, Territorial, or Municipal citizenship— both in order to meet the single citizenship requirements of your States and to put an end to any presumption that you are acting as a "Federal Citizen".

This Declaration / Re-Conveyance placed on the Public Record prevents the British and/or Municipal Bunko Artists from claiming that you are in any sort of "insurrection" against their government —how can you be in "insurrection" against a foreign government? —and the knowledge that everyone in your group is similarly declared to be an American State Citizen discourages them from pursuing the sorts of obstructive infiltration they are famous for.

There are also a substantial number of groups out there who are trying to restore and reconstruct the "missing" Federal States of States that should be making up the Federal Branch of the Federal Government. These efforts need to be redirected, because those attempting them don't have the standing to do what they are trying to do.

Like virtually everyone else, the members of these groups are "considered to be" Federal Citizens until they declare otherwise, and can be accused of "insurrection" against the existing Territorial Government or Municipal Government if they are at the same time trying to rebuild the Federal States of States that belong to the American States.

The Missing Federal States of States doing business as, for example, The State of Georgia, literally belong to Georgia and the People of Georgia, meaning the members of the State Jural Assembly. Nobody else has any right to say "Boo!" about The State of Georgia and nobody else can "reconstruct" it, either, no matter how well-meaning these efforts may be.

You have to reclaim your lawful standing as

an American State National and take action as an American State Citizen before you can reconstruct the Federal State of State that belongs to you and your State. You have to be acting in the correct capacity and with the correct standing or it can't be done.

The People of Georgia — the Jurors and Members of the Georgia Jural Assembly, standing firmly on the land and soil of Georgia, that actual State — have to reconstruct the Federal entity dba "The State of Georgia".

So all these misbegotten efforts being undertaken by various other groups of people claiming to represent the Federal States of States are doomed from the outset thanks to ignorance, and they remain subject to attacks by the Territorial and Municipal Branches of the Federal Government, because the people mounting the reconstruction effort "appear to be" British Territorial Citizens or Municipal CITIZENS engaged in activities that might be construed as harmful to the Territorial or Municipal Governments.

The British Territorial and the Congressional Municipal Governments aren't necessarily looking forward to the reconstruction of the properly functioning States of America, even though they are obligated morally and contractually to honor our right to freely "assemble" and can't keep us from reconstructing the Federal States of States, so long as we are acting in our true character and capacity as American State Nationals and American State Citizens.

Pass the word to the other groups that are attempting to do the work of reconstruction. Explain how it is that only the "People" — the members of the State Jural Assemblies — declared to be State Nationals and State Citizens, are able to enforce the provisions of the Federal Constitutions, and likewise, why only the "People" populating the State Jural Assemblies are enabled to act in the International Jurisdiction to re-construct the Federal States of States.

Please note that Members of Jural Societies "inhabit" their watery International Jurisdiction of the Sea, while members of State Jural Assemblies "populate" their International Jurisdiction of the Land and national jurisdiction of the soil. They are "Persons" and we are "People".

For All The Jural Assemblies – 24

The American Government

Our American Government created the Federal Government.

That may be big news for some people reading this, because generations of Americans have been purposefully left in the dark and conditioned to glaze over when any topic of history is discussed — much to their detriment.

Our American Government precedes the existence of the Federal Government by over ten years and in part, by more than thirty years, and it far exceeds the Federal Government in authority, power, and standing. Even now.

By Maxim of Law, the creation is never greater than the creator.

Our American Government is meant to control and use the Federal Government as an "instrumentality" and that instrumentality was never meant to serve the interests of any foreign government— though thanks to disloyal politicians and corrupt generals, it has served the interests of both the British Empire and the Holy Roman Empire to the detriment of our People and States.

The Constitutions were used to create all three branches of the Federal Government: Federal, Territorial, and Municipal. When you understand that fact you are prepared to hear, perhaps for the first time in your lives, that there are three (3) Constitutions, not one:

The actual Federal Constitution is The Constitution for the united States of America.

The Territorial Constitution is The Constitution of the United States of America.

The Municipal Constitution is The Constitution of the United States.

These entities were specifically created to exercise nineteen (19) of our own enumerated powers for us. That is to say, all branches of the Federal Government were created to act as subcontractors to do work for us in foreign jurisdictions, and to provide us and our States with stipulated services on a mutual basis.

The work to be done by the three branches of the Federal Government falls into three categories — (1) the General Business of this country in the realm of International Commerce, (2) the Military and Territorial Property Management Business which was farmed out to the British Territorial United States, and (3) the Municipal Business which was left in the care of the Pope and the Holy Roman Empire.

Very little mention of our actual American

Government is made in any of the Constitutions, for the simple reason that we and our American Government are not the subjects of these venerable documents. The Constitutions each concern themselves with structurally setting up and delineating the rights and duties of a specific branch of the new Federal Government and say little or nothing about our pre-existing American Government which is doing the setup.

We are referenced in the Preamble of each Federal Constitution as "We, the People", and we are implied throughout the Bill of Rights Addendum. We appear strongly in Amendment X, and in tiny bits and pieces of almost apocryphal nature elsewhere, but "We" and our American government are simply not the subject of the Constitutions.

For this reason, people who are looking to the Constitutions to provide information about our American Government are bound to be disappointed for the period of time and the documents related to our formal set-up are outside the purview of such Seekers.

The roots of our American Government go back to 1756 and the onset of what is called in America "The French and Indian War" which is known in Europe as "The Thirty Years War". It was in that conflict that Americans like George Washington tasted what it was like to be used as mercenary troops by the British— you fight the war for them, and then you pay for it, too.

It was also during that time period and just prior to it, that Washington — the largest private landowner in America and a direct close relative of the British King — became aware of the disastrously limited treaties the British had made with various Native tribes.

According to those Treaties, the Colonists were never supposed to encroach upon the land beyond the Cumberland Gap. Washington had seen the richness of the Kentucky Wilderness and the Ohio borders. He knew that the Colonies would need to expand and that those Treaties had to be overcome— and it would be to the advantage of both the Colonists and the British King if they were dispensed with. But how?

By a change of government.

It would no longer matter what the "Great Father Across the Water" said in his Treaties with the Natives, if he was supplanted by a violent Revolution and the rise of a new government headed by the Colonists, albeit, a government secretly loyal to the King and to British interests in America, a government headed by Washington and internationalists like Franklin, who supported the even-then-Globalist agenda of the Holy See.

To put it bluntly, then as now, Britain conspired to avoid its responsibilities and maintain its good name — yet retain control — by installing a puppet government. Ours. Then as now, greed and deceit were fundamental components of the scheme. This was the 1776 version of the "New Deal" in which the Natives lost their Treaties and King George regained access to a whole continent — all without dirtying his gloves or soiling his reputation by obviously and openly defaulting on his earlier treaties.

Washington would do the defaulting for him and be none the worse the wear, because Washington never agreed to the Native treaties in the first place.

So let's take a look at how this new American Government was structured and when and how it was created and exactly who "We, the People" are.

There are three principal jurisdictions of law that were defined and set up by the Holy See hundreds of years before the American Revolution: air, land, and sea.

Our American Government was set up on this pattern, too, with a separation of duties and functions according to air, land, and sea jurisdictions of the law.

During the five years 1776-1781 numerous new entities, which we would now call "governmental units", were set up.

First, the original colonies were redefined as landed estates and formed a union of these estates by Unanimous Declaration as of July 1, 1776 (published July 4, 1776) known as The United States.

Then, shortly thereafter, September 9, 1776, the estates created States for themselves–another level of governmental organization and another Union of these States called The United States of America.

Thus we have the people of the soil (county) jurisdiction populating their estates, for example, virginia, and we have their union of soil jurisdiction states doing business as The United States. Each such state forms a separate nation of people living within its borders: Virginians, New Yorkers, and so on.

We have the same people operating in the international jurisdictions of land and sea (international capacity) as People and as States, for example, Pennsylvania, and we have their Union of States doing business as The United States of America.

Each State forms a separate Nation (for the purposes of international business) composed of the People living within its borders, and together the People operate as The United States of America.

Thus, finally, we know who "We, the People" are: the living population of the estates doing international business as States (separately) and as The United States of America (mutually). This is the level of American Government which gave rise to the three-branches of Federal Government and which defined the structure, duties, and obligations of the Parties under the Constitutions.

There was one other "union" of governmental units formed as part of the initial set up of our American Government — just as the states created the States to function for them in the realm of international affairs on both land and sea, the States chartered incorporated "States of States" to function for them in the realm of global affairs and commerce —that is, business conducted between two incorporated entities.

The States thus formed their States of States to function for them in the global jurisdiction of the air and specifically, in the jurisdiction of International Commerce. This then created a union of States of States known as the States of America under The Articles of Confederation, effective March 1, 1781— more than six years prior to the adoption of any Constitution.

This, then, is the American Government which existed prior to any Constitution:

The United States — a union of geographically defined soil jurisdiction estates (states) formed by and deriving from the original colonies.

The United States of America — a Union of geographically defined States formed to serve the people and states in the international jurisdictions of land and sea. This is the original Federation of States.

The States of America — a union of inchoate, chartered, and incorporated States of States formed by the States to serve the States and People of The United States of America in the global jurisdiction of commerce. Each "State of State" such as The State of New York is called a "Confederate State" and the Union they form is established under The Articles of Confederation. This is the original Confederacy or Confederation of States.

All of this was organized during the height of the Revolutionary War and long before the existence of any Constitutions. This is the American Government that created the Federal Government.

Please notice that two of the American Unions and their member states/States are geographically defined, actual and factual entities with borders, and physical assets.

The United States claims and controls the top six inches of soil. This is our National jurisdiction and the instrumentality responsible for it.

The United States of America claims and controls the land underlying the soil, as well as exercising the duties and rights owed to the States in the international jurisdiction of the sea. This is our International jurisdiction and the instrumentality responsible for it.

The third Union of States of States, known as the States of America, is composed of members like The State of New York, which are not defined geographically. They exist only on paper and are chartered by our States as incorporated entities engaged in International Commerce.

This is our Global jurisdiction and the instrumentality that is supposed to be responsible for it –but, thanks to legal chicanery and fraud following the so-called American Civil War — this Union of States of States has been moth-balled since 1868, and our American Government has been hobbled ever since.

Part of your mission as Members of your State Jural Assemblies will be to re-charter your Federal States of States, like The State of Georgia, and The State of Maine, to take over the General Business functions of the Federal Government.

For All The Jural Assemblies – 25

State Nationals, State Citizens, and State Electors

Okay, let's try it again:

State Nationals = everyone born within the physical geographical borders of a State. A National has no particular duty to serve the State other than to obey the Public Law (Non-Statutory Law) and keep the peace.

State Citizens = those State Nationals who additionally choose to serve the State Government in some capacity, such as Jurors, Militia Members, elected officials, or hired officers.

State Electors = those State Nationals who own land in the State and meet other requirements such as legal age, etc., to participate in State Elections.

You can be either: (1) a State National or (2) a State Citizen.

Being a State National or a State Citizen does not necessarily mean that you qualify to be a State Elector. You can be part of the State Jural Assembly and serve as a Juror without being a State Elector. You can be elected to a Public

Office, such as Sheriff, without being able to vote for yourself.

This is because of the pesky issue of letting non-landowners vote on questions that only affect landowners, and therefore the requirement that State Electors be landowners.

For All The Jural Assemblies – 26

The National Jurisdiction: Soil

In our discussion of the American Government that we are heir to, we identified three "unions" of various kinds of "states" that existed long prior to the creation of the Federal Government.

They were and are:

The United States — a union of soil jurisdiction "landed (e)states" formed by the former colonies via Unanimous Declaration issued July 1, 1776, published July 4, 1776. This is our "national jurisdiction". Each state has defined geographical boundaries.

The United States of America – a federation of Land Jurisdiction States formed September 9, 1776 for the purpose of joint operations in international jurisdiction, including the international land and sea jurisdictions. This is our "international jurisdiction". Each State has defined geographical boundaries.

The States of America — a confederation of inchoate "States of States" formed under The Articles of Confederation, March 1, 1781, for the purpose of conducting the business of the States in "global commercial jurisdiction". These "Federal States of States" have no defined geographical boundaries and exist only on paper. (These are the "Missing" Federal States of States.)

Please note — all this is our American Government, which existed prior to and which created the Federal Government as an "instrumentality" to provide services to the States and People of this country.

Let's look briefly at our "national jurisdiction" — the soil jurisdiction of each state in The United States.

Imagine the familiar outline of your State of the Union. Got it?

Now pretend you are slicing it like a layer cake horizontally, taking the top six inches of the soil off. It has the same outline and shape, but not much depth.

This is your state's national soil jurisdiction.

We call all the rest underneath the soil "the land". The land is also shaped exactly like the outline of your State of the Union, but it is a much thicker layer, miles deep, and it forms your State's international land jurisdiction.

Together we call this "the land and soil" of your State of the Union. The two jurisdictions — the national soil jurisdiction state and the international Land Jurisdiction State — are both geographically defined and both work together hand in glove.

So, what does the "national" soil jurisdiction of your State do and how does it operate?

The first thing it does is guarantee local control.

This is the level of the "state republics" and "republican states" guaranteed by the constitutional contracts.

The soil level states are seldom referenced in print, but when they are, they appear in all small letters: maine, virginia, florida, etc. These are the member states of The United States.

When we are born we all enter the world via the soil jurisdiction of our state, and are in the political status of a "man of the soil" known as "jus soli" or a "state national".

This determines our basic nationality. We are, for example, "virginians" and because we are "virginians" we are also considered "Virginians". This, in turn, identifies us as "Americans" for international purposes.

When we are born, we are not "citizens" of anything.

Being a "citizen" implies an obligation to serve a government. It is patently ridiculous to claim that a newborn baby has an obligation to serve any government, nonetheless, certain disreputable governmental services corporations have made exactly such claims against babies born in America for several generations. This is part of what we need to address.

It is the "jus soli" status of the baby that leads to the political status at the State level of State National. Neither one have any obligation to serve any government at all; they are required to obey the Public Law and keep the peace and other than that, they are free as birds.

The basic dictum of the national soil jurisdiction is, "Harm none and be harmed none."

Likewise, the republic states and their state republics are seldom referenced in print and even more seldom are they officially populated and used to conduct business — but they can be. This results in a quorum of state nationals opting to act as state citizens, and invoking the national soil jurisdiction of their State of the Union to conduct national-level business.

For these purposes, Texas is a nation. Pennsylvania is a nation.

The soil jurisdiction also includes surface water, so each state republic also has a republic of state attached to it, and for business purposes, you have "The Texas Republic" operating the soil jurisdiction of Texas and "The Republic of Texas" operating the surface water jurisdiction of Texas.

All of these entities are unincorporated and operate as unincorporated businesses.

They are owned and operated by the people who are native to Texas and those who have been "naturalized".

Naturalization at the State level is a process of having a home inside the borders of the State for at least a year and a day, without committing any felonies or taking public assistance, and firmly declaring on the public record your desire and intention (after meeting the basic requirements) to make that State your permanent home.

In the old days, this was done by taking out three small ads in the local papers over a period of 90 days, and there is still no obstruction to doing this now. In this way, a guy from Florida can adopt Texas as his home, for example, or a "U.S. Citizen" born in Croatia or Washington, DC, can become a Minnesotan.

Obviously, the soil is like the skin on a body. By owning and controlling the skin, the local people retain the vast majority of the power of government if they act in their proper capacity and organize to do so. Everyone is standing on the soil, so the power of arrest basically belongs to the soil jurisdiction and the republican state authorities and their county/County Sheriffs.

However, operating the Soil and Land jurisdictions of our States of the Union requires us to foreswear and expatriate from any other citizenship, including any federal citizenship.

Most Americans do not realize that they have been kidnapped on paper into a foreign jurisdiction and misidentified as either "United States Citizens" or "Citizens of the United States" or "US CITIZENS" almost from birth, a circumstance that keeps us from actually owning land and controlling our own assets.

In fact, most States of the Union became severely de-populated prior to this current effort, simply because people didn't realize that they were the victims of unconscionable contracting activities by their own employees.

Coming home to the "land and soil" of your State means that you are eligible to inherit all that you have been deprived of, that you come under the Public Law, instead of any private "Statutory Law", that you can exercise local control of your land and surface water resources, and that you can operate your "republican states" —that is, the national soil jurisdiction of your State of the Union, again.

So long as you see the advantage of doing so and educate yourselves and declare your birthright political status— and work with others of like-mind to restore the "land and soil" jurisdiction government owed to this country— there isn't a power on Earth than can stop you from inheriting and controlling what is rightfully yours.

For All The Jural Assemblies – 27

International Jurisdiction

One of the most important things to remember is that in America and for purpose of the American Government, the word "interstate" is completely synonymous with the word "international". This is because each State is, in fact, its own country and its own nation.

For the sake of streamlining certain functions and creating uniformity in some areas to bulwark our strength (such as military operations and expenses) and to expedite free trade (such as interstate banking services) our States have agreed to act together as members of an unincorporated Federation of States known as The United States of America — but each and every "power" that this Holding Company has or can delegate derives from the member States and powers which they intrinsically possess. And the member States remain sovereign.

As we saw, the national soil jurisdiction is controlled by unincorporated republican states which are members of The United States.

The international jurisdiction is controlled by unincorporated States which are members of The United States of America, a Federation of States

The international jurisdiction controlled by your State has three components, air, land, and sea.

We have discussed the international land jurisdiction of the States briefly and described it generally as the thick layer of rock and material underlying the top six inches of soil. Land obviously includes your State's mineral and groundwater resources. The international land jurisdiction of your State is also able to appear in some contexts above the soil — as it does when we build railroads and post roads and post offices and interstate highways and interstate electrical services.

These are transit lanes and service stations on land analogous to sea lanes and docks in the jurisdiction of the sea– resulting in routes and infrastructure that have been created to deliver interstate/international or global services within your State. Because this interstate/international infrastructure is within the borders of your State such facilities remain under State control, but because of their international nature and their role as part of the connecting service web other States depend on, they fall under your State's international land jurisdiction and function under international law.

Both the railroads and the post offices have been used to promote various in-roads against local law and control. Many States have allowed these foreign international entities to exercise the right of Eminent Domaine, for example, which allows them to "condemn" public and private property –essentially commandeering it– to allow construction of infrastructure.

Thus, these enterprises have been allowed to abuse both public and private property owners for their own benefit using the excuse that the Public Good they provide outweighs the loss to other's property rights.

Similar arguments have been advanced with less success to excuse the imposition of "property taxes" on landowners within each State to pay for public services, such as snow removal on pubic roads. This places a disproportionate and arbitrary burden on the landlords that is nonconsensual and is, in fact, an unlawful conversion of property rights.

The Territorial State of State that is functioning in a "care-taking" capacity and mandating these practices in our States of the Union has no actual authority to impose upon the States and People in this way, and instead of presuming upon the landlords should be paying back dividends and lease fees and compensating the States and People for the use of their resources.

An examination of the Comprehensive Annual Financial Reports of each Territorial and Municipal State-of-State organization reveals that the income these organizations receive from the use of our State resources each year is far in excess of all expenses and that largesse should, logically, be available to pay for public services such as snow removal and fire departments without any additional taxation. However, without active and competent input from the State Jural Assemblies, the For-Hire State of State employees and their corporate legislatures have padded their own pension plans instead.

The Checks and Balances System has been totally out of whack in this country because the State Jural Assemblies have not been meeting regularly, have not weighed in on the deployment of State income, have not protected private property rights, have not insisted on the enforcement of the Public Law, and haven't been doing their job representing the interests of the actual State and People.

Also, because these interstate/international businesses are operating in international jurisdiction but are interfacing directly with our State's soil jurisdiction, there are conflicts of law that result.

The most visible part of this conflict of law arises from the fact that these private and international business organizations functioning under international law have been allowed to employ "Pinkertons" — private law enforcement agencies — within the boundaries of each State, and these LEO organizations have proliferated and been hired as subcontractors in other venues to substitute for actual peacekeeping officials and officers.

Law enforcement officers are, generally speaking: (1) not familiar with the Public Law, having been trained to enforce the "code and statutory law" of the international jurisdiction instead; and (2) are not properly directed to enforce the Public Law, even when they are hired to do so.

These private security agencies have become abusive and have failed to recognize the fact that the People of the State are living under the Public Law and, except when they are actually on a train, in a post office, or otherwise in direct contact with these limited international land jurisdiction functions—railroads, electrical power line right of ways, post offices, etc., the living People of each State are not subject to international law within the boundaries of their States.

Territorial State of State employees and Municipal STATE OF STATE employees, are subject to international law, but the States and People are not — until and unless we directly interface with a railroad, post office, or other interstate/international utility — for example, we rob a Post Office, vandalize a power pole, or commit murder on a railroad right of way.

The Territorial and Municipal organizations in each State have discovered that they can make money by arresting people and filling up prison facilities, which has led to the proliferation of more and more oppressive statutory "laws" and burgeoning prison populations.

This Prisons for Profit scheme is a direct affront to our sovereignty in which People of each State are deliberately mischaracterized as Territorial or Municipal "Persons", held to be subject to Territorial and/or Municipal international law, and incarcerated at our expense. This is not only an abuse of our People, it is an abuse of our Purses by our employees.

They are profiting themselves by arresting us under color of law, charging us under statutory laws we are not naturally obligated to obey, and then charging our States for the service of putting us in jail.

More abuses include registration and copyrighting of our private Given Names as property belonging to State of State and/or Municipal STATE OF STATE organizations, conferring of Federal citizenship obligations via unconscionable contracts, seizure, manipulation, and patenting of our unique DNA, securitization of living people as assets belonging to these organizations, and the bonding of public and private property belonging to our States and People for the debts of these "state of state" organizations.

These are actions readily recognizable as crimes that have been going on in our country for decades via the abuse of our State's international jurisdiction.

This has only been made possible because our trusting people have been deliberately kept unaware of the false claims being made against them by their employees, and our State Jural Assemblies have not assembled and kept watch on the proverbial store.

The international sea jurisdiction belonging to each State varies according to the individual State's location and geography. Thanks to the Great Lakes and abundant large navigable rivers, plus sea coasts on three sides of our country, most States have ample and direct access to the transport of goods and services via these natural conduits.

Generally speaking, the British Monarch is supposed to be acting as the Trustee of all Americans and all American shipping on the High Seas and Navigable Inland Waterways, and as such, our States should not have a great deal to worry about — however, as more and more Americans have unwittingly allowed themselves to be mischaracterized as Territorial or Municipal "citizens" instead of reclaiming/retaining their birthright political status, the British Monarchs have been encouraged to escape their duty owed to the States and People, and eager to profit themselves from the States of States and Persons, instead.

The Coast Guard owed to each seaboard State has been allowed to run amok and been privatized and misdirected similar to what has gone on with the hired law enforcement officers being used to substitute for peacekeeping officials and Officers of the Law. As a result, the Coast Guard has become a clearinghouse for smuggling and theft from the States and People instead of a bulwark in our defense.

Port Authorities have similarly been employed in the interests of international crime and exportation of Americans, both literally and figuratively, along with our resources, using ports of entry and "Free Trade Zones" established in virtually every State.

The international air space owed to each State has similarly been abused to favor international business interests and placed the profits of these commercial interests above any benefit owed to the States and People of this country. We are constantly bombarded with false advertising and propaganda from foreign sources clogging up our public airwaves, and no effort is being made to impose any better standards.

Media monopolies have become common and other monopolies have grown up uninhibited by the proper application of Public Interest anti-trust and anti-monopoly legislation. Although these issues often bridge upon commerce rather than international trade, the State Jural Assemblies have a potent voice that needs to be heard in Washington, DC, and elsewhere.

hat goes on in our States is fundamentally under the authority and control of the People of each State, so this is all hash that we need to settle with our employees and service providers and international Trustees.

In order to do our job, we have to choose to act in our birthright political capacity as one of the People of our State of the Union, and make public declaration of this fact by recording our deliberate and permanent expatriation from any "presumed" federal citizenship obligation.

If we fulfill our obligations as State Nationals and/or State Citizens and/or State Electors, we will have more than enough to do.

The members of our State Jural Assemblies have the critical role and function of nullifying unconstitutional and repugnant laws, upholding and enforcing the Public Law including the Constitutions, and controlling the soil (national) and land (international) jurisdictions of our State.

Beginning with the fact that we are not acting as Federal "Persons" and are not accepting any Federal "citizenship" obligations, for all the reasons cited above and far more beyond the scope of this small discussion, our State Jural Assemblies must act to direct the proper administration of the international land jurisdiction we are heir to, and to bring effective complaints to our federal service providers and international Trustees regarding the misuse and abuse of the international sea and air jurisdiction of our States.

As brief as this discussion has been, the issues raised are compelling and should be enough to convince any American that effective action must be taken to restore the People and the States and the Public Law.

For All The Jural Assemblies – 28

Global Municipal Jurisdiction

We could also call this section "From Trade to Commerce".

When we engage in "peaceful national and international trade", this is a private and natural right held under our own authority. This is the realm in which we are supposed to use our "Good Name" also known as "Given Name" also known as "Trade Name" — the name that our Fathers and Mothers gave us at birth.

We are naturally unincorporated and sovereign entities when we stand on the land and soil of our geographically defined states/States; however, when we venture into the international jurisdiction of the sea or upon the navigable inland waterways to engage in trade with corporations or people from other countries, we are considered to be acting as "Foreign Situs Trusts" temporarily under the care of the British Monarch who owes us safe passage, aid, and assistance — so long as we are claiming our birthright political status as American State Nationals or American State Citizens.

If, however, we allow ourselves to be misrepresented as Federal Citizens of any sort, no such guarantees apply; the same Name applied to a Federal Citizen may be mistaken for a "stateless Person" — and stateless Persons can be attacked, salvaged, and plundered under the Laws of the Sea.

So, how does this work? All Federal Citizens are "stateless Persons" of one kind or another, because their "states" are all "inchoate states" — incomplete, non-physical, incorporated franchises of —from our perspective— foreign governments and foreign commercial corporations.

These corporate franchises are foreign, first and foremost, because they are not functioning as people. They are functioning as legal fiction "Persons".

The instant that your State National political status is stolen from you as a baby, and your Good Name is misidentified as that of a "US Citizen", you are labeled as a "Federal Citizen" and deprived of all the protections and guarantees and property rights you are heir to. You and your estate can be pillaged and salvaged, and the Queen, who is supposed to be acting as your Protector won't say a thing; indeed, she will laugh all the way to the bank.

This is because Federal Citizens have no Natural and Unalienable rights and their inchoate States (properly called "States of States") are not Parties to our Constitutions and other Treaties with Great Britain.

Only the actual geographically-defined States and physical People have access to the constitutional guarantees as intended. States of States and Incorporated Persons are not generally "covered" by these agreements.

So when we claim our proper birthright political status as American State Nationals or American State Citizens, our business is our own on the land and soil of our State, and when we venture out in the wider world, we are under the protection of the British Queen.

If we do not claim our proper birthright political status and wind up identified as a Federal Citizen of some kind, we are considered temporary residents on the land and soil of our own State, we are unable to actually own our own land, and we have no constitutional guarantees — only duties to perform.

This circumstance above all others underlines the advantage and importance of claiming/retaining your birthright political status.

This is just the first round — what happens to us when we are innocently engaging in international trade and are mistaken-accidentally-on-purpose for Federal Citizens; there is another level to this same basic identity theft/misrepresentation scam that occurs when we enter the global realm of commerce and are "mistaken" for fully incorporated entities: PERSONS.

In the international land jurisdiction where

our States of the Union naturally abide, there are no living people; instead, we function as People — State Citizens are functioning as Officials and Officers of our States — Jurors, Sheriffs, Justices, Electors, and so on, while State Nationals function as Inheritors and may also be Electors.

In the global municipal jurisdiction there are no people, either, just fully incorporated commercial corporations chartered by various governments, operating under the names of people, e.g., JOHN PHILIP SOUZA, as well as more familiar commercial corporations like GENERAL ELECTRIC.

The Municipal Jurisdiction is Global in nature and is organized as separate Municipalities that operate as International City States and charter all these fully incorporated commercial corporations. Municipal Jurisdiction is also called the "Empire of the City", meaning Rome under the auspices of the Holy See, and since 1929, Vatican City, which has set up and operated all the Municipal Charters on Earth.

This model of government is based on the plenary oligarchy of Ancient Rome, under the Caesars which established independent City-States and Roman Territories throughout the world.

The Municipality of Washington, DC is set up as a plenary oligarchy run by members of the

Municipal United States Congress under Article 1, Section 8, Clause 17. It is an independent, international City-State created under a Municipal Charter doing business as "the" United States, run in turn by a Municipal Corporation, doing business as the Municipal Corporation of the District of Columbia. The District of Columbia itself is meanwhile operated as a Territorial Democracy doing business as "the" United States of America.

Similar independent international City-State organizations have been chartered all over the world, some of the principal members that boast their own flags are the Municipality of Washington, DC, the Inner City of London, Vatican City, the United Nations, and the City of New York. These chartered municipal entities engage in international affairs and international trade, and then go one step further and charter franchises for themselves known as commercial corporations, or PERSONS.

Thus, the Municipal Corporation of the District of Columbia, a "doing business name of" the Municipality of Washington, DC, an independent international City-State doing business as the "United States" (Incorporated) has chartered the UNITED STATES, CANADA, DETROIT, JOHN PHILIP SOUZA, WESTMINSTER, PENNSYLVANIA....over a 185,000 such Municipal franchises, plus, via its UNITED STATES franchise and its STATE OF MAINE and STATE OF TEXAS and other franchises—– hundreds of millions of "individual franchises" named after each and every one of us, have been created without our knowledge or consent.

The Global Municipal Jurisdiction is the realm of Commerce— which is business between two fully incorporated entities— meaning that these entities are not just "Legal Fictions". They are LEGAL FICTIONS created and chartered by other Legal Fictions/LEGAL FICTIONS and are another step or two or three removed from the realm of actual living people.

A wide variety of Legal Persons can participate in International Trade, including unincorporated Mom and Pop American businesses called doing business under State National and State Citizen Names like "Lisa Ann Purdue" or "John's Autobody Shop" or US Citizen Names like "John George Walton".

Without firmly declared provenance recorded (Americans) or registered (US Citizens also known as Federal Citizens) the capacity in which any Person is acting is left up to presumption.

Not surprisingly, the Queen's Territorial henchmen have chosen to "presume" that we are not acting in our birthright capacity, are therefore owed no protection and no constitutional guarantees. They have deliberately falsified the evidence in their favor by registering our Names and leaving us clueless that any of this was going on and equally clueless that we needed to declare and record our birthright political status as Americans.

The Municipal Government has been just as busy registering its own franchises in our NAMES.

As a result, we can, if we so wish, operate as British Territorial CITIZENS under the Spanish laws of the Commonwealth of Puerto Rico or we can operate as Municipal CITIZENS under the laws of the Municipality of Washington, DC…. or as Citizens of the United States (Municipal Franchise) or as United States Citizens (Territorial Franchise) or we can say "No" to all this fraudulent undisclosed identity theft and operate as we are meant to operate, by declaring our natural birthright political status, exercising our own country's sovereignty, and enforcing the actual Constitution owed to us.

Please note that the Municipal United States is specifically limited to the ten miles square of Washington, DC, and the purpose of letting Congress run the City as a plenary oligarchy in the first place was to provide an equal meeting ground — not to launch a competing "commercial" government made out of paper and hot air and false claims in commerce.

The responsibility for these travesties lies both upon the members elected to serve "as" delegates to unstipulated "Congresses", and upon the foreign governments and governmental services corporations that have allowed, promoted, and profited from these activities.

The unrestrained corruption of the Municipal United States Congress is also the particular responsibility of the Roman Catholic Church and the Holy Roman Empire which issued the Municipal Charter(s) and failed to oversee them. As this is written, many key Municipal Charters have been revoked and the offending corporations have been or are being liquidated for cause; however, the same guilty parties running these crime syndicates as "service organizations" have been allowed to re-apply for new Municipal Charters and to shelter their ill-gotten gains, so that a true Good Faith correction is lacking.

By substituting foreign corporate franchises — in effect, their own "Persons" / "PERSONS"— to replace and usurp upon the living American People, our States, and our lawful Persons, these criminals have endeavored to steal our identities one-by-one, to falsely indebt us and accrue debt against our public and private assets, to set up a gigantic national mortgage fraud, and to embezzle trillions of dollars out of our country's economy

Again, although this is a summary discussion, it should be clear to any American that there is compelling reason and advantage in reclaiming and retaining our birthright political status as American State Nationals and American State Citizens—- and very significant adverse consequences from allowing anyone to consider you a Municipal CITIZEN, as all Municipal CITIZENS are by definition debtors, criminals—- and slaves because they are criminals.

See the 13th and 14th Amendments to the Territorial Constitution made by the Scottish corporation doing business as "The United States of America" (Incorporated) in 1868.

For All The Jural Assemblies – 29

The Confederation of States

Both the word "state" and the word "of" need special attention when we read.

The word "state" can represent a multitude of things. It can refer to a state of mind, or the soil jurisdiction of your natural state, or your landed State of the Union, or, as too often happens, the word "state" can be used as shorthand for something that properly needs to be called a "state of state".

We have the Federal "States of States" also being called "Confederate States" almost from the moment The Articles of Confederation were signed in 1781.

Please duly note this confusion and know that "Confederate States" are not "States" in the same way nor existing in the same jurisdiction as our land jurisdiction "States". They are instead "States of States" which are entirely fictional and disconnected from the world of fact.

The word "of" creates a separation between "States" like Maine and "States of States" like The State of Maine, which was the original Federal State of State for Maine. That is also to say that The State of Maine was the original Confederate State created under The Articles of Confederation in 1781, two years before the end of the Revolutionary War.

About now we have people scratching their heads. What? Confederate States during the Revolutionary War?

Yes. Contrary to what most of us have been taught or left to assume, Confederate States, more properly and less confusingly called Federal States of States, existed and operated long before the so-called Civil War.

In the case before us, the word "of" also implies ownership. The State of Maine (a Confederation State) belongs to Maine (a Federation State) and Maine belongs to the People of Maine.

A State of State is not a State. It's a State "of" (belonging to) a State.

A State of State is a commercial business entity operating in the Global Municipal Jurisdiction. It is pure legal fiction — a fiction created by a fiction. In this case, Maine created The State of Maine.

Let's review the process:

The living people of a state come together to form a State Jural Assembly, and this group operating in the capacity of "People" — that is, elected Officials, hired Officers, Jurors, and Electors of the State Jural Assembly– create their State, for example, Maine.

"Maine" is a complete State, because it is not entirely fictional. The State of Maine is called an "incomplete State" or an "inchoate State" because it is entirely fictional, having no express material boundaries or location in space.

Maine is geographically defined and has substance and assets. At the same time it is "corporate" and a legal fiction in the sense that it has a fictitious and arbitrary Proper Name: "Maine" only stands for the land and soil of Maine because that is the name the People of Maine chose to call their estate. They could have chosen to call their estate "Wamsutta" and we could have The State of Wamsutta to deal with instead.

So…..

The United States is composed of unincorporated republican states like "wisconsin", doing business as The Wisconsin Republic (national soil) and The Republic of Wisconsin (national surface water), and it is populated by living people using Proper Names like: James Woodby.

The United States of America is composed of unincorporated but "corporate" States like Ohio, doing business as Ohio (international land and sea) and is inhabited by the People of Ohio, that is, living people acting as Lawful Persons, and populated by these Lawful Persons using Proper

Names like: James Allen Woodby.

The States of America is composed of incorporated States of States like The State of Pennsylvania, doing commercial business in the global municipal jurisdiction of the air.

The state (soil and surface water) gives rise to the State (international land and sea) which gives rise to the State of State (global municipal jurisdiction).

The people of a country populate its soil and surface water jurisdiction and they give rise to the People, Lawful Persons, populating States operating in the international jurisdiction of the land and sea, and thence, the Lawful Persons give rise to Legal Persons inhabiting States of States operating in the global municipal jurisdiction of the air and commerce.

Actual living people acting as Lawful Persons create States, but States then create States of States populated by Legal Persons, so at each stage of this process we observe increasing "fictionalization".

We go from actual and factual to airy fairy in three basic steps: state > State > State of State, and from living person to Lawful Person to Legal Person in the same three steps.

As you will note, the State level is the last connection to the actual, factual world we know. After that, its all fiction and fictions creating more fictions, spinning off endless "doing business as" Legal Personas.

It's in this completely fictional realm of the global municipal air jurisdiction that the States of America was created to function in 1781. The members of this "perpetual union" of "Confederate States" were "States of States" belonging to our States and operating in the global municipal jurisdiction of the air—in commerce.

The Confederation of States, more properly, The Confederation of States of States, doing business as the States of America as of March 1, 1781, was composed of commercial businesses owned and operated by our States.

Maine owned and operated The State of Maine.

Virginia owned and operated The State of Virginia.

Georgia owned and operated The State of Georgia...

This is the way our American Government was already set up as of 1781, and with a little alteration caused by the adoption of the Constitutions, this is the way it was structured until after the Civil War when the Federal States of States went "Missing in Action".

For All The Jural Assemblies – 30

The Constitutions

Just as it is a shock for many people to realize that there is an American Government operating separate from the Federal Government it created, and that there were "Confederate States" in operation long before the Civil War, it will come as a shock to many to realize that there are in fact three (3) Constitutions, not one.

Much of our education has been neglected so as to promote fraud against us and make us — and our entire country — easy marks.

Let's notice a few general things that are important about the Constitutions and the Federal Government they created.

1. The word "Federal" can be used in several ways. It can be used as a descriptive adjective indicating a contractual relationship with our American Federation of States — The United States of America [the unincorporated version] — or any other federated entity; it can also be applied to any part of a federated entity.

This is important, because it allows a great deal of "genial deception" and not-so genial deception, which we will discuss a bit more fully.

2. All "Federal" entities referenced by the Constitutions operate exclusively in the global municipal jurisdiction of the air and are fictions created by fictions.

Via the Constitutions, these commercial businesses contracted with our States to provide our States with nineteen (19) stipulated services, which according to the Preamble of each Constitution, includes safeguarding our National Trust.

That is, there is no direct connection between any Federal entity and our States, except that our States own and (are supposed to) operate the Federal States of States, which have been officially Missing in Action since 1868, and all the Branches of the Federal Government are under contract to provide our States with stipulated services.

3. There are three (3) branches of the "Federal Government" established by the three (3) Constitutions, and they are all limited and related to each other within the context of their separate constitutional agreements with our States:

(a) The Federal Branch of the Federal Government is supposed to be run by the Federal States of States (the original Confederate States) and their Union of States of States doing business as the "States of America" operating in the global municipal jurisdiction of the air — commerce.

(b) The Territorial Branch of the Federal Government is run by the British Government under authority delegated to King George III via the Treaties leading up to and including The Definitive Treaty of Peace, Paris, 1783, which ended The Revolutionary War.

This Territorial Branch of the Federal Government is in charge of supervising British Territorial Citizens "residing" in our States of the Union for the purpose of providing us with stipulated governmental services— most especially, protection on the High Seas and Navigable Inland Waterways (Naval Defense and Defense of our Commercial Fleets and International Trade) and management of our "Territorial Possessions"— like the Insular States of Puerto Rico, American Samoa, and Guam, and the Territorial States arising under the Northwest Ordinance, which provides an orderly means for new territories of The United States to become States of The United States of America.

(c) The Municipal Branch of the Federal Government is supposed to be operated by members of the Federal Congress, and the Federal Congress is supposed to be composed of Deputies from each State charged with running the Federal State of State belonging to their State of the Union. The Municipal Branch of the Federal Government is given the responsibility to oversee the District of Columbia as a neutral meeting ground and to provide a local government for the Municipality of Washington, DC.

Unfortunately, they were granted plenary power over the ten miles square of the District of Columbia and the Municipality of Washington, DC. See Article 1, Section 8, Clause 17. And the Municipal Charter was granted by the Holy Roman Empire.

So, contrary to what you learned in Eighth Grade, the Branches of the Federal Government are not "executive, legislative, and judicial", they are Federal, Territorial, and Municipal.

All three operate in the global municipal jurisdiction of the air and are operating as commercial business enterprises providing governmental services.

All three have separate existences apart from their role as service providers under the constitutional agreements.

All three are obligated by solemn treaties and commercial service agreements to provide Good Faith Service to our States and People.

All three operate exclusively via Delegated Powers.

In order to provide us with the nineteen (19) stipulated services, our States delegated some of their "powers" to be exercised by the Federal Government — with the complete understanding that they retained all their other powers (Amendment X) and also with the understanding that if the Federal service providers failed to hold up their end, the States and People doing business as The United States of America, would have the right to sever the constitutional agreements, withdraw their Delegated Power, and find new means of providing the stipulated services and doing business in the commercial realm.

This is precisely where we stand today, the urgent reason that the State Jural Assemblies must assemble, and the reason our birthright political status must be declared and asserted.

Only the People who own the States that contracted with the commercial businesses operating the Federal Government are competent to (a) restore and reconstruct the Federal States of States and (b) enforce the constitutional agreements.

As things now stand, those of us who woke up early in the morning are operating the Holding Company, The United States of America. We have fully informed the rest of the world that all bets are off and that we are only accepting services explicitly stipulated by the Constitutions and only on a month-by-month quid pro quo basis while our States Assemble.

We have also informed all Parties that incompetency in bankruptcy severs the presumed service contracts and related delegated authorities by Operation of Law, and that we acknowledge and accept the bankruptcy of the Municipal United States and receive back all Powers delegated to the Municipal Congress.

Once the people have been sufficiently educated and have reclaimed their birthright political status and taken up their Lawful role as People and have Assembled their State, a Continental Congress of the States and their Lawful Deputies will be called to confirm and reconsider all aspects of the history and the situation going forward.

Meantime, be advised:

1. The actual Federal Constitution is called: The Constitution for the united States of America, adopted in 1787. All members of the "States of America" organization are Federal States of States, also called "Confederate States" which have been mothballed since 1868.

2. The Territorial Constitution is called: "The Constitution of the United States of America" adopted in 1789 — notice the small "the". This version of "United States of America" is a British commercial corporation operated as a "Territorial Democracy"— which has been running the Federal District Government in the "absence" of our own Federal States of States— not be confused with our American Federation of States doing business as The United States of America.

3. The Municipal Constitution is called: "The Constitution of the United States" adopted in 1790. Notice that there is no reference to "of America" involved. Notice also the small "the"

as part of "the United States" — this municipal commercial corporation is not to be confused with The United States representing our republican states.

In an ideal world, the States of The United States doing business as The United States of America own and operate the Federal States of States (also called Confederate States), and the Territories naturally belonging to The United States are administered by British Territorial subcontractors prior to their inclusion as States in The United States of America federation, and the only Municipal Government in this country is controlled and limited to stay and operate exclusively within the District of Columbia by the Territorial Government.

You can now see how very far we have strayed and how potentially catastrophic this situation is without your prompt attention and participation in your own history and your own State Jural Assembly.

At the very beginning we noted that because the word "Federal" can be used in many contexts and can be applied to any part of any federation, it lends itself to various kinds and levels of deception.

In the course of this 150-year debacle, both the Territorial and Municipal Governments have represented themselves as "the" Federal Government and they have been allowed to do so because they are part of the Federal Government. This, then, has led everyone to assume that the actual Federal Government in sum total, including the Federal Branch of the Federal Government, was still in operation long, long after the Civil War ended and the Federal States of States were due to be "reconstructed".

Also, other entities having commercial contracts with either the Territorial or Municipal Governments, like the Federal Reserve, have made a "claim by association" to be "federal" entities, when in fact they have no relationship with the Federal Branch of the Federal Government, nor with our Federation of States doing business as The United States of America.

The Federal Reserve is as "federal" as Federal Express. So is the FBI.

For All The Jural Assemblies – 31

Mandatory Citizenship Requirements

As we have learned and reviewed to this point, the American Government is composed of three unions of three different kinds of states: soil, land, and inchoate Federal States of States.

The United States = soil jurisdiction states and people, geographically defined, republican states, State Republics and Republics of States.

The United States of America = international land jurisdiction States and People, geographically defined, members are Ohio, Maine, Florida, et alia.

The State Jural Assemblies create and operate and populate these geographically defined States of the Union and together constitute "We, the People".

The States of America = global municipal jurisdiction States of States, not geographically defined, "inchoate", legal fictions, members are: The State of Ohio, The State of Maine, The State of Florida, et alia.

These are not States in the same sense as land and soil jurisdiction States. They are commercial corporations operating in the global municipal jurisdiction of the air as "States of States".

The Persons operating these "States of States" create State of State Jural Societies instead of State Jural Assemblies.

The land and soil jurisdiction States require us to have a single citizenship and allegiance — to them. They don't allow any form of Dual Citizenship and never have.

The Founders adhered to the principle that 'no man can serve two masters" and did not allow conflicted people (people with conflicts of interest, such as loyalty to the King) to participate in State Government.

Thus, obviously, you do need to expatriate from any other citizenship if you want to participate in a State Jural Assembly.

And if you want to continue to claim Dual Citizenship as a Federal employee or dependent, you are welcome to set up a State Jural Society, and operate in that realm and continue to do the political party hokey-pokey.

America as a whole needs help from both sides of the fence, but there is a fence, and we need to be aware of it.

The main fact to take in is that the actual geographically defined States don't allow any wishy-washy on this issue of citizenship requirements for participation in State Jural Assemblies, so anyone who doesn't want to expatriate from "US citizenship" needs to set up and participate in a State Jural Society instead.

Please note that for purposes of foreign travel, Americans are under the auspices of The United States of America (the unincorporated version) not The United States.

Federal employees and dependents are under the auspices of "the" United States when they travel and are considered Municipal Citizens while abroad, subject to global Municipal Law.

For All The Jural Assemblies – 32

The Federal States of States

As we have learned in the prior articles about the Union of soil jurisdiction states, and the Federation of States and the Confederation of States of States, there are fundamental misunderstandings and semantic deceits we need to overcome—things that we have been taught that were wrong, things that were half-truths, and assumptions that we made that need correction.

The first consideration is that the word "states" can refer to a lot of different things and we should not just assume that our geographically defined States are being referenced, because people often sloppily refer to "States of States" as "States", too, and don't always understand that actual States are defined geographically.

The second is that the word "federal" can be similarly misapplied. It can refer to our Federation of States doing business as The United States of America, or it can refer to some other "federation" entirely.

The worst bit of confusion of this sort surrounds the Federal States of States, which have also been called "Confederate States" since The Articles of Confederation were signed in 1781.

We need a thorough understanding of the Federal States of States, aka, Confederate States, before we discuss the American Civil War.

The first thing we notice is that "Confederate States" also known as the Federal States of States have been around since long before the Civil War. This comes as a big surprise to most people.

The second thing we notice is that these Federal States of States, also known as "Confederate States" are "inchoate" states, that is, they are total legal fictions and they are not geographically defined.

The third thing we see is that The States of States are commercial corporations created by the State Governments. Each Federal State of State is chartered and run by a State. Georgia chartered The State of Georgia, for example.

The fourth important thing is that the original Federal States of States were all named using the same style of Proper Name and they all capitalized "The" and included this definite article as part of their names: The State of Georgia, The State of Maine, The State of Minnesota…..and so on.

The fifth important point is that all these Federal States of States, also known as Confederate States, were members of the States of America union— one of the three unions of "states" making up the original American Government as of 1781.

The sixth important take-home message that their Union of States of States, doing business as the "States of America" is the Union being referenced in the Preamble of the Constitutions. In other words, it's the States of America Confederation that is the "Union" being "perfected" by the Constitutions, not The United States, not The United States of America.

The actual Federal Constitution is called, "The Constitution for the united States of America".

Please note that this is the "original' and "controlling" constitution in the series of three, the one that creates and defines the "Federal Government" as of 1787.

Note also that the word "united" is used as a descriptive adjective and is not part of the Proper Name of the States of America organization being referenced, and notice that "the" is not capitalized or included in the name, either.

This further underscores the fact that these Federal States of States and their States of America organization are operating exclusively in the realm of global municipal commercial jurisdiction.

Article VI of all three "federal" Constitutions

guarantees that debts and obligations of the Confederacy will continue to be honored under the new power-sharing arrangement established by the Constitutional Convention.

The adoption of the Federal, Territorial, and Municipal Constitutions basically split up the business service contracts and gave part of what was originally all being done by the States of America to the British Territorial Government and the Holy Roman Empire's local Municipal Government doing business as "the" United States.

We can be sure that: (1) the original Federal Constitution known as "The Constitution for the united States of America" directly references the "States of America" Confederation; (2) this is the "Union" being "perfected" by the adoption of the Constitutions; (3) Article VI references honoring the debts and obligations of the Confederate States —because they are the only ones being impacted by the adoption of the Constitutions.

Take note — part of the commercial business of the original States of America Confederation is being given away to the British and the Holy Roman Empire as a result of adopting the Constitutions.

For All The Jural Assemblies – 33

The American Civil War

From our discussions we have now fully realized that the Constitutions and the Federal Government arising from these venerable agreements only affected our country's operations in the municipal jurisdiction's realm of commerce — that is, business conducted between two fully incorporated, chartered legal fiction entities.

Adoption of the Federal, Territorial, and Municipal Constitutions didn't affect our soil jurisdiction estates, doing business as The United States, nor did they impact our land jurisdiction States doing business as The United States of America, but they did change the operations of the States of America, a union of commercial corporations chartered by the States.

The impact of the Constitutions on the States of America and on the member commercial corporations doing business under names styled like this: The State of Pennsylvania — was dramatic.

The most important immediate change was that control of our fledgling Navy, and our Naval operations were ceded to the British King, who was obligated to function as our Trustee on the High Seas and Inland Waterways, and to protect our private and international and commercial interests in those venues.

Control of our international trade policy was also given away to the King. At least in the realm of commerce, we traded our freedom for safety, though it is doubtful that many Americans realized this at the time.

The overall result of adopting the Constitutions was to split up the functions originally taken care of by the States of America, and assign some of them to foreign governments to take care of "for" us.

This power-sharing concession was pre-destined by the Treaties and earlier agreements that allowed for the end of The Revolutionary War. In other words, these concessions and promises to share power with the British King and the Holy Roman Empire were obligations our Forefathers accepted as part of the Peace Negotiations and the Constitutions that resulted — Federal, Territorial, and Municipal — were simply the instruments used to implement the pre-existing deal.

So, the States of America remained the fundamental Federal Service Provider as we came out of the Constitutional Convention, and as of 1787, The Constitution for the united States of America, emerged as "the Federal Constitution". That is, this is the Constitution creating the Federal Branch of the Federal Government.

Though its powers and turf were battered and beaten in this process. the States of America was still a very potent force, with responsibility for the nation's money and many other key services.

The loss of control of the Naval Powers and the loss of control of our international trade policy was grievous, but was deemed necessary at the time: coming out of the Revolution we had a huge commercial fleet, but almost no Navy. We had lots of raw materials to ship to eager markets in Europe and a need to get paid for them, but our unprotected commercial fleet was being decimated by privateers.

Most of the American-based private commercial fleet belonged to two groups — British American former colonists sailing out of Rhode Island and Massachusetts and Virginia, and Dutch New York and Southern interests derived from the "disappeared" Dutch East India fleet that mysteriously vanished circa 1702 and wound up in New York and the Pacific. They were the primary movers insisting on the surrender of our Naval Powers so that they could continue their commercial shipments unmolested.

The rest of the people were tired of war and accepted the new inroads against our sovereignty rather than continue to fight and starve.

Still, for many, these losses remained a sore point and the adoption of the Constitutions was by no means unopposed— nor, were the losses unforgotten.

As the British Parliament began to impose ever-more disadvantageous trade policies on the American Federal States of States — all commercial corporations with their own axes to grind– and tempers flared.

Malfeasance by British Merchant Marine Officers known as Bar Attorneys led to the War of 1812, which was a push-back against unequal trade policies and unfair tariffs and market rigging.

In 1819, the States of America responded by toughening already existing constitutional provisions against conflicts of interest and "buying of loyalty" by foreign powers bestowing foreign "Titles of Nobility" on Americans. This was applied to the practice of bestowing the title "Esquire" on American Bar Attorneys.

Frustrated by our resistance to their interference and manipulation of our commercial interests to our own detriment, the British Monarch and the then-Pope signed a clandestine treaty known as The Secret Treaty of Verona, in 1822, in which they agreed that our American system of government was intrinsically opposed to both feudal monarchies and papal authority.

In gross Breach of Trust, they agreed to secretively undermine our government — a course of action which they have pursued ever since and which has finally led to the present circumstance.

This is the Big Picture, but to further understand, we must necessarily revisit what has euphemistically been called "The American Civil War".

First one must ask — what is a "Civil" War as opposed to any other kind of war?

Civil = City = Municipal = Global Commercial Jurisdiction = war between Persons, not People = war between commercial corporations.

This "War" called "The American Civil War" was not properly termed a war, but was instead a "Commercial Conflict" like the Vietnam Conflict, fought by foreign mercenaries on our shores, and by employees and volunteers backing the various Federal State of State commercial corporations.

Those Federal States of States that remained loyal to the original Confederation doing business as the States of America represented the North and were called "Union" troops. Many Americans even at the time mistook which "Union" they were fighting for and in what context.

The Federal States of States that broke away from the original Confederation and formed their own version doing business as The Confederate States of America, represented the Southern

State's commercial corporations, and their troops were called "Confederates" as a result.

The King of England gleefully funded both sides of the conflict and the separate international City State of Westminster lost no time setting up effective blockades and conscription services and issued privateer licenses against all our shipping North and South.

From the standpoint of the Monarchists and the Holy Roman Empire, the object of the American Civil War was to defeat the South and take Southern Cotton out of the European markets, permanently end the cost-saving advantages that slavery provided the Southern Plantations, and to reduce the Northern States of States to a condition of bankruptcy. They succeeded in all respects.

And Americans and America paid for it all.

You must remember what we are talking about — a commercial "war" for markets and profits, waged by commercial corporations that are essentially no different than any other commercial corporation except that they are chartered directly by actual States instead of being chartered secondhand by States of States.

The British and French-backed Northern States of States resented slavery for profit and market reasons, so they encouraged the Abolitionists. Private slavery was already out of fashion in Europe and of no great economic consequence to their domestic markets— except that it gave the American Southern States of States a cost advantage in the marketplace, and they competed against British and French cotton plantations established elsewhere in the world.

The British and Holy Roman Empire backed Southern States of States favored slavery for profit and market reasons, so they encouraged the Pro-Slavery Plantation owners — many of which produced products other than cotton. Remember that the addictive properties of high nicotine tobacco were just beginning to be exploited as a de facto drug trade prior to the Civil War, and the squabble over cotton production interfered with tobacco, sugar, rum, molasses, and many other products.

Last but not least, this commercial "war" was a bonanza for the railroads, the arms manufacturers, and the U.S. Armed Forces, especially the British-controlled Navy, which received privateer kickbacks. There had never been a better opportunity for professional soldiers in this country and men like Ulysses S. Grant and William Tecumseh Sherman made the most of it.

So it is not a pretty picture, but it is an accurate one. The members of the original Confederation of Federal States of States doing business as the States of America —- all of them commercial corporations chartered by their States, all of them assigned service contracts under The Constitution for the united States of

America — took the European bait and went to war with each other.

By 1863, the Northern States of States were bankrupt. By 1865, the Southern States were in ruins and the Southern States of States gave up the fight.

Since it was not an actual war according to the definition of "war", there was never any Declaration of War issued by any Congress related to the American Civil War, nor was the surrender of Lee's Army at Appomattox a peace treaty. The corporations and those backing them simply decided to stop fighting and went home, leaving the Federal Government in chaos that has persisted and been capitalized upon until this day.

The Federal States of States are separate entities though they were all chartered by the actual States. The Confederation of States founded in 1781 was in ruins. It would require a concerted effort to "Reconstruct" the Federal States of States and form new commercial corporations to service their obligations under The Constitution for the united States of America.

That job of reconstruction of the Federal States of States has never been accomplished, and it can only be done by the actual States and People.

So the People must assemble and the States must assemble and they have to take care of long-overdue business. As we shall see, certain parties who owed us better service left us unaware of this urgent necessity and deliberately lulled us into the assumption that the Reconstruction Era was long over, and that we had no work to do.

Until this long overdue process of reconstruction is undertaken, the entire Federal Branch of the Federal Government is out of commission, moth-balled, and the assets of the original Federal States of States that came through the ruination and bankruptcies have been rolled into "land trusts" — meaning that these trusts belong to the land jurisdiction States and People.

The assets of The State of Maryland and The State of Maine and The State of Pennsylvania…. and so on, have been rolled into the Maryland State (land trust), Maine State (land trust), Pennsylvania State (land trust)….

The actual States and People of this country are being summoned to take action in their own behalf and to reconstruct their Federal States of States and to restore the Federal Government they are owed—- all of it, not just the Territorial and Municipal bits.

Please bear in mind and be aware that your actual soil jurisdiction states, dba The United States, and your land jurisdiction States, dba The United States of America, and all their member republics and States, have never been involved in any of this commercial uproar.

Our only duty and our only failure thus far is to recognize certain semantic deceits, to organize ourselves into competent State Jural Assemblies, and to re-charter our Federal States of States to provide the services owed to our States under The Constitution for the united States of America.

For All The Jural Assemblies – 34

Reconstruction: Your Mission

Strange as it may seem to us today, the Reconstruction required as a result of the Civil War has never been finished. In truth, it was never properly started. No adequate Notice and Disclosure of the circumstance was ever given to the general populace of America. And there are obvious, self-interested reasons for that.

Let's take a step back and look at the close of the Civil War.

We have now properly understood who the parties to the armed conflict were: commercial corporations owned and operated by the States went to war with each other. These entities operated as, for example, The State of Ohio, The State of Florida, The State of Wisconsin and so on, chose sides and fought, but this was a private sector quarrel among corporations — as if General Electric and Westinghouse hired mercenaries and solicited volunteers and got into an armed conflict in the middle of the village green.

As such, it was a patently illegal and lawless event, and by definition, there could be no actual Declaration of War, no Peace Treaty, and no actual Victory.

The idea behind The Articles of Confederation was to create an internal alliance of "capital business interests" devoted to the welfare of all the States and People. This is why The Articles of Confederation which sought to bind together the commercial corporations operating as an "instrumentality" of each State in the global municipal jurisdiction overseen by the Office of the Roman Pontiff, proposed to be a "perpetual" union.

From the very first, it was realized that if commercial interests were in conflict such that The States of States opposed each other, and this schism was allowed to spread far enough, it would endanger the entire country. So the Founders were at pains to impress upon The States of States the necessity of working together for the common good and maintaining the perpetual union of the original Confederation —and a united front in the global municipal jurisdiction.

Unfortunately, agent provocateurs — as we now know, members of the Rothschild banking cartel and other European banking interests — kept watch for an issue that might create such a schism between The State of State commercial corporations, and they found it: slavery.

The last Congress of the Federal States of States adjourned for lack of quorum when the Southern States of States walked out. The Deputies known as "United States Senators" who were essentially the CEO's and Fiduciaries of these commercial corporations could no longer conduct business.

The remaining Delegates representing the Northern commercial corporations collaborated with the British Territorial Government to continue operations under the guise of acting to "preserve the Union" and "the Constitution" — meaning the Territorial Constitution and its role for the British King as Trustee over our Naval and Trade and Commercial activities.

The entire "war" was fought by colluding American commercial corporations and foreign interests and had nothing to do with our actual States and People, except that the conflict was fought illegally on our soil, many of our people were killed, maimed, and otherwise harmed, the Federal State of State commercial corporations were decimated, and the British-backed Territorial Branch of the original Federal Government installed itself as a military junta.

Even Ulysses S. Grant was stunned when, after the end of the hostilities, he arrived in Washington, DC, and realized the extent of the manipulation, corruption, and hypocrisy involved in promoting the Civil War. As a man and a soldier, he had been sure of his moral cause throughout the actual fighting, only to discover that slavery was never the actual issue at all, and that those who now claimed victory were intent on creating a new kind of slavery: public slave ownership, instead of private slave ownership.

What remained was this: the Northern Federal States of States — commercial corporations owned and operated by the Union side of the conflict were bankrupt and in reorganization. The Southern States of States — also commercial corporations owned and operated by the Confederate States were bankrupt, too, but never sought bankruptcy protection. A British Territorial Military junta was in control of Washington, DC, and soon puppet governments installed by force in the South would send Territorial Delegates to Washington.

These Territorial Delegates would join their colluding Northern brethren who had operated in the same Territorial capacity throughout the war to operate a British Territorial-level "Congress" as a substitute for the Federal Congress.

There were still enough people left alive who knew the truth and who wished to restore our rightful Government, so numerous attempts were made to do so.

President Andrew Johnson did what he could to protect the States and People by formally declaring the land jurisdiction at peace, three times, in public. (May 10, 1865 – April 2, 1866 – August 20, 1866)

Members of the Territorial "Rump" Congress admitted the circumstance by passing the "Reconstruction Acts". These were undertaken as "emergency" measures by a foreign military government — essentially, an American "Raj" — to maintain control over the civilian population during a transition back to normal government operations.

That transition has never taken place. The vast bulk of the Reconstruction Acts have never been repealed and are still in full force and effect.

The Reconstruction Acts which were supposed to be temporary measures violated the original Constitutions at least five different ways, but the three most immediate violations did three things that we still struggle with today.

Article IV, Section 4 was violated when, under the Reconstruction Acts of the Territorial Congress, the actual Southern States were denied their republican form of government and control of their own soil jurisdiction after the end of the "war".

Article I, Section 8, Clause 17 was violated by the Territorial Congress unlawfully exercising exclusive legislative power outside their Districts.

Article IV, Section 3 was violated when the Territorial Congress formed Territorial "States of States" to replace and substitute for the Federal States of States.

The sum total result of all this is that the Federal Government — three levels of subcontracting commercial corporations that are supposed to be providing our States and People with Good Faith Service — have been operating unlawfully and illegally ever since.

Remember that there are in fact three Branches of the Federal Government, all composed of either our own or foreign commercial corporations in the business of providing governmental services:

Federal Branch = The States of States chartered by our States, like The State of Maine, The State of Iowa, etc. These self-chartered commercial corporations are supposed to be providing us with all goods and services stipulated under the Constitutions except for those services noted below:

Territorial Branch = British King acting as Trustee of our private, trade, and commercial business interests on the High Seas and Navigable Inland Waterways; caretaker of our Territorial holdings.

Municipal Branch = Holy Roman Empire -commercial jurisdiction, supposed to be controlled by the Territorial Government and limited to the ten miles square of the District of Columbia, with plenary control of the Washington, DC Municipality. Supposed to provide a safe meeting ground for commercial business and uniform laws and standards for the conduct of such business.

After the Civil War, only two out of three Branches of the Federal Government remained in operation. The primary and most important subcontractor, the Federal Branch, was never "reconstructed".

Instead, our primary contractor, the States of America organization was knocked out of commission, left disorganized (reconstruction never took place), and the secondary British Territorial subcontractors secretively usurped in and substituted their own Territorial "States of States" in 1868.

We have been operating on two wheels instead of three, our guys have been cut out of all the juicy government contracts since 1868, and as a result, the Brits and the Popes have been in illegal and unlawful control of our Federal government ever since.

The substitution of British Territorial "States of States" for American Federal "States of States" was accomplished via similar names deceit (fraud). The average people were left unaware of any change. To them and to their eyes, there was a "State of State" government before the war and after. The switch from The State of Georgia to the State of Georgia passed them by.

In the same way, the switch from the unincorporated American Holding Company doing business as The United States of America — which is another level of our American Government entirely— was deliberately confused by the introduction of a Scottish commercial corporation doing business as "The United States of America, Incorporated" as of 1868, so as to illegally access our credit and make it appear that we were bankrupted, when in fact no unincorporated entity is eligible for bankruptcy protection.

This is all identity theft of the same kind that occurs when a credit card hacker illegally accesses your accounts.

The Popes who were supposed to be running the Holy Roman Empire/Office of the Roman Pontiff and policing commercial operations worldwide— and who are obligated by treaty to act as our Trustees in the Global Jurisdiction of Commerce— sat on their velvet tuffets and did nothing to stop it. Instead, they happily profited themselves and helped organize the expansion of the fraud.

The British Kings ordered the members of the Territorial Government to keep mum about it — see 18 USC 472. The military was told that all this was a matter of "National Security".

What it is really a "matter of" is gross Breach of Trust, Treaty Violations, Theft, Embezzlement, Fraud, Inland Piracy, Racketeering, and other

Crimes by Treaty Allies against the interests of the American States and People.

Your Mission as members of your State Jural Assemblies and as members of your State Assemblies proper, is to reclaim your stolen identity as American State Nationals and American State Citizens and to Assemble your State and finish the Reconstruction.

Only you have the power to re-charter your Federal States of States and retrieve their assets– that is, all the State land trusts doing business under names like: the Wisconsin State, Ohio State, et alia., from the Territorial Caretakers.

Only you can put the American subcontractors back in place and in control of the services we are owed by the "Federal" Government.

One of the great ironies is that in spite of all the evidence of fraud, bad faith, the use of similar names deceits, rampant identity theft, securities fraud, and other crimes committed by our purported Trustees and Allies against us, they still attempt to blame us and say that it's all our fault because we didn't boot up new Federal States of States after the Civil War.

Well folks, lets put that complaint to rest, act in our actual capacity as State Nationals and State Citizens, and do the work of Reconstruction—- create our own American Subcontractors to do the principal share of work as assigned under the actual Federal Constitution.

The People of each one of our States need to charter their State's commercial corporation under their own State's sovereign authority, and then join as a member of the States of America— – a perpetual union and Confederation of States of States serving as the Federal Branch of the Federal Government.

That will put an immediate end to a lot of monkey business and leave nobody any cause to complain about our action to take back control of our country and its assets and its service contracts.

Also, acting as the People, as members of our State Assembly and our State Jural Assembly, we can address the multitude of international crimes which have been practiced against us.

For All The Jural Assemblies – 35

Lawful Persons

It is important for the State Jural Assemblies and the State General Assemblies, which follow, to understand the concept of "Persons".

A "person" is created every time we name someone or something, be it a baby or a business— every time we create any form of office, job title, military rank, pen name, married name, performer's name or nickname, too.

A person is not a living being. Your name is not you. It is a "handle", a "utility", a means of identifying you among billions of other people. It is a "representation" or "image" or "persona" of yours, that you are supposed to own and care for in the same way that you own a bicycle.

Your Proper Name, also called your Good Name, your Trade Name, or your Given Name (because it is given to you—literally) is your Lawful Person when you are standing on the land and soil of your State.

Persons fall into three basic categories: (1) unincorporated, (2) corporate, and (3) incorporated.

The first two kinds of Persons—unincorporated and corporate — are "Lawful Persons". The distinction between unincorporated and corporate is based on the degree of separation from physical actuality.

Unincorporated Lawful Persons are sometimes called First Degree Sovereigns and Corporate Lawful Persons are considered Second Degree Sovereigns.

Sovereignty is an element of free will and it is only possessed by Lawful Persons; only unincorporated entities are truly free.

So we each have our own Proper Name, which is a Lawful Person—sometimes referred to as a "Natural Person".

Private unincorporated businesses are another class of Lawful Persons known as "Business Persons". These also naturally occupy the land and soil jurisdiction of the American States.

A third kind of Lawful Person is called a Corporate Business Person — not "incorporated" — merely "corporate".

A Lawful Corporate Business Person is typically formed by one or more unincorporated businesses. Unions, Leagues, Clubs, Holding Companies, Fellowships, Federations, and some forms of Trusts are Lawful Corporate Business Persons.

Our unincorporated state republics joined together to form the unincorporated union of states doing business as The United States.

The United States is a "Lawful Corporate Business Person" called a "Union" doing business for other businesses— the member state republics.

The United States of America is also a "Lawful Corporate Business Person" called a "Holding Company" doing business for other businesses — the member States.

All Lawful Persons are unincorporated entities. All Lawful Persons can freely conduct domestic trade and international trade on the land or sea.

Lawful Persons are of a different class and kind of Person than Legal Persons.

It's important to know that the entire actual American Government is unincorporated and populated by Lawful Persons.

When you return "home" to the land and soil of your State of the Union, you do so as a Lawful Person. When you act as a State Citizen and as a member of your State Jural Assembly, you do so as a Lawful Person.

It's equally important to know that the Federal Government — all three branches of it: Federal, Territorial, and Municipal — is incorporated and inhabited by Legal Persons, instead. All Federal Citizens whether defined by Article 1 Section 2, Clause 2 or Article 1, Section 3, Clause 3 or by the 14th Amendment are acting as incorporated franchises or agents or officers of commercial corporations and are acting in a different capacity and a separate jurisdiction. We shall treat Legal Persons as a separate topic.

The American Government is composed of Lawful Persons and the Federal Government is composed of Legal Persons.

This is an important distinction and deserves your careful thought, notice, and consideration.

The Bible, which is the source of Land Law throughout most of the world, takes a dim view of "persons" and "personages" —- criticism which is largely addressed to officials bearing titles, royal persons, and legal persons who fail to live up to their duty:

Acts 10:34

Then Peter opened his mouth, and said, Of a truth I perceive that God is no respecter of persons:

Psalms 26:4

I have not sat with vain persons, neither will I go in with dissemblers.

Job 13:10

He will surely reprove you, if ye do secretly

accept persons.

James 2:9

But if ye have respect to persons, ye commit sin, and are convinced of the law as transgressors.

Proverbs 28:21

To have respect of persons is not good: for a piece of bread that man will transgress.

Psalms 82:2

How long will ye judge unjustly, and accept the persons of the wicked?

Proverbs 24:23

These things also belong to the wise. It is not good to have respect of persons in judgment.

Proverbs 28:19

He that tilleth his land shall have plenty of bread: but he that followeth after vain persons shall have poverty enough.

Zephaniah 3:4

Her prophets are light and treacherous persons: her priests have polluted the sanctuary, they have done violence to the law.

Proverbs 12:11

He that tilleth his land shall be satisfied with

bread: but he that followeth vain persons is void of understanding.

Ezekiel 27:13

Javan, Tubal, and Meshech, they were thy merchants: they traded the persons [Slaves] of men and vessels of brass in thy market.

Ephesians 6:9

And, ye masters, do the same things unto them, forbearing threatening: knowing that your Master also is in heaven; neither is there respect of persons with him.

Lamentations 4:16

The anger of the LORD hath divided them; he will no more regard them: they respected not the persons of the priests, they favoured not the elders.

Malachi 1:9

And now, I pray you, beseech God that he will be gracious unto us: this hath been by your means: will he regard your persons?saith the LORD of hosts.

1 Peter 1:17

And if ye call on the Father, who without respect of persons judgeth according to every man's work, pass the time of your sojourning here in fear:

1 Timothy 1:10

For whoremongers, for them that defile them-selves with mankind, for menstealers, for liars, for perjured persons, and if there be any other thing that is contrary to sound doctrine;

1 Samuel 22:22

And David said unto Abiathar, I knew it that day, when Doeg the Edomite was there, that he would surely tell Saul: I have occasioned the death of all the persons of thy father's house.

These are murmurers, complainers, walking after their own lusts; and their mouth speaketh great swelling words, having men's persons in admiration because of advantage.

James 2:1

My brethren, have not the faith of our Lord Jesus Christ, the Lord of glory, with respect of persons.

2 Chronicles 19:7

Wherefore now let the fear of the LORD be upon you; take heed and do it: for there is no iniquity with the LORD our God, nor respect of persons, nor taking of gifts.

Deuteronomy 10:17

For the LORD your God is God of gods, and Lord of lords, a great God, a mighty, and a terrible, which regardeth not persons, nortaketh reward: [Work for free in other words, as 'everything acquired by the Slave/Person is acquired for the Master']

Colossians 3:25

But he that doeth wrong shall receive for the wrong which he hath done: and there is no respect of persons.

Jonah 4:11

And should not I spare Nineveh, that great city, wherein are more than sixscore thousand persons that cannot discern between their right hand and their left hand; and also much cattle?

Deuteronomy 1:17

Ye shall not respect persons in judgment; but ye shall hear the small as well as the great; ye shall not be afraid of the face of man; for the judgment is God's: and the cause that is too hard for you, bring it unto me, and I will hear it.

Deuteronomy 16:19

Thou shalt not wrest judgment; thou shalt not respect persons, neither take a gift: for a gift doth blind the eyes of the wise, and pervert the words of the righteous.

Romans 2:11

For there is no respect of persons with God.

Many thanks to my friend in Australia, Cameron -McGregor/Mukunda, who compiled the above list of Bible references about persons and shared with me, as I share with you.

APPENDIX

Letter to Destry and the National Assembly Effort in Total

Ignorance cannot be allowed to carry the day, nor any arrogant idea that our actions will not be subject to the most rigorous kind of international and global review — because they will be and must be.

All Jurors of all State Jural Assemblies must Declare their political status as exclusively that of State Citizens, because our States do not allow any form of Dual Citizenship. Period.

This means that each and every State Jural Assembly Juror must "Expatriate" from any presumed Federal, Territorial, or Municipal United States citizenship.

You cannot ride the fence or "leave it till later" and there are two very good reasons for this:

(1) As long as people don't formally and explicitly renounce Federal, Territorial, and Municipal citizenship(s) and embrace their natural birthright State Citizenship— those same foreign governmental entities can hold them to be in insurrection against their foreign government and arrest them.

This is the scenario that so many people fear

and which they try to avoid by pussyfooting around about their political status— which is precisely what they cannot do, if they wish to avoid being harassed and arrested and mischaracterized in the same way that the Bundys and LaVoy Finicum and the Colorado 9 have been.

So, either declare your only "citizenship" to be State Citizenship, or get out of the position of being an administrator organizing a foreign government (from the federal perspective)— ours.

You will be doing yourself a big favor as well as everyone else involved. We do not need another big spectacle of patriots being harassed because they are stupidly trespassing against federal entities, or acting in "insurrection" against governments that they don't owe allegiance to in the first place.

Stop soft peddling and blurring the lines and giving the Federales any excuse to object to the States and the People assembling.

2. In order to conduct business for the States and the People of this country no member of the State Jural Assembly may be acting in conflict of interest, which is evidenced by trying to maintain any Dual Citizenship obligations. If we conduct our elections or charter a new Federal State of State, the people doing so must have the proper standing and be acting in the right

capacity, or all our efforts are null and void from the start.

Spaniards cannot conduct the business of the Irish Government and if that is not perfectly obvious to everyone, it should be.

Our actions in these regards will be examined by international authorities and any group not functioning properly and in the right capacity will have their votes thrown out. That is, the elections of our State Jural Assembly will be tainted by including votes from others who are still acting as "Persons".

The validity of the entire effort can be destroyed by just a handful of people acting in Bad Faith or ignorance and failing to Declare their sole citizenship as State Citizens.

The onus and responsibility for checking everyone's Expatriation and keeping proper records is on the State Jural Assembly organizers. And at least some of the responsibility for encouraging and guiding the State Jural Assemblies lies upon the National Assembly organizers.

I want this issue of mandatory Expatriation from Federal citizenships well and thoroughly understood by everyone, for their own sakes and safety going forward, and for the validity and standing of our actions as a whole. I suggest that everyone read Article 24 in the For All The Jural Assemblies Series, subtitled "The American Government" for further insight into which government it is that we are responsible for, and which in turn is responsible for reform and restoration of the Federal Government.

The Tale of Two Governments

There are two (2) Governments— the American Government and the Federal Government.

The American Government created the Federal Government.

The State Jural Assemblies are part of the American Government, not the Federal Government.

A Person (Federal) cannot function as one of the People (American).

Now, most Americans don't realize that they have been signed up as Federal Citizens, and shanghaied and misidentified as British Territorial Citizens and/or Municipal United States Citizens, but that is what registration of all those Birth Certificates accomplished.

You have been secretively signed up as a member of their clubs, held to all their membership obligations, forced to pay all their fees and dues — and all without your conscious knowledge. You've also been "deemed" to have "voluntarily" given up all your constitutionally protected rights and guarantees and to have given up all your material interests as a "gift" — a donated "decedent estate"— for the benefit of their clubs.

And all this has been done "for" you by your Federal Employees, who then benefit themselves at your expense.

To get back home and be recognized as an American, you have to declare your actual birthright citizenship and claim it — and that means revoking and expatriating from the foreign Federal citizenship that has been "conferred" upon you and which you have been unknowingly occupying almost all your life, since a few days after your actual birth.

Many of you are balking about giving up Federal Citizenship and expatriating from it, because you don't know how beneficial it is to you and your country for you to do so. You assume that you are losing something precious, when in fact, you are letting go of the chains that bind you and the false claims that have impoverished and oppressed you.

You are naturally part of the American Government, not the Federal Government-— and in order operate the American Government you are owed, you have to declare your "return" to your birthright citizenship as an American State Citizen and expatriate from any form of Federal Citizenship.

It would be against international law for any Federal Citizen to occupy a public office of one of our States, and against the law of the Territorial and Municipal United States for anyone "deemed to be" a Federal Citizen to interfere with the operations of any other Federal agency.

There have been some people suggesting that "Anna is telling us what to do." and they are pridefully bridling up like little kids claiming to be King of the Sandbox. They think this is an issue of pride and authority. It's not.

If a judge knows that you are in a situation that you don't fully understand and that you may already be acting in violation of law or skating on the edge of such violation—- and that judge fails to sound the alarm and explain the situation to you—- then they are culpable for your death or other misfortune.

The Watchman must give the alarm. And so must the Watchwoman.

In the course of my life, I have often had to sound the alarm. I have had to explain this particular point of law and history more than once. And far from it being an issue of pride, it is an issue of grief.

Each time I raise my hand and spell it out, there is some bonehead in the crowd who thinks he knows it all — and he says, "Oh, she's just a woman! Come on, boys! We'll do it our way! This is our country! Blah-blah-blah-blah-blah…"

And every time people get off track and led into the woods by these Pied Pipers, good men and women suffer, they get hauled into federal prisons, they get attacked by IRS agents, they get ambushed by their own employees.

Ask Bruce Doucette. Ask Cliven Bundy. Ask LaVoy Finicum. Ask Randy Weaver.

If you think that you don't have to listen to what I am telling you and don't have to declare your political status and don't have to expatriate from Federal citizenship to be part of your State Jural Assembly — think again.

Praying without words

You can get there via physical pain or emotional, either one.

Those of you out there who have been in this extreme state know that in such misery, it isn't even possible to talk.

Words will not form.

Instead, what happens, is a great emptiness, as if the pain purges everything else and leaves you at the very ragged edge of consciousness — and still. Absolutely empty and still.

At that moment, in that state, you are suddenly perfectly lucid and at peace. Your mind is still and yet aware.

The constant blaring of voices, your own and everyone else's, is also stilled.

You have reached the mountaintop where there is nothing but you and your Father, the One Life that gives rise to all life and all consciousness.

And you discover that there is no need to say anything, no barrier between you. He knows everything — the "all" of it — without a single word being formed.

And you realize that you are loved beyond all telling and accepted just as you are.

You become aware of the direct connection you have with the Living God and you let yourself go— just flowing into that infinite love and energy like a river flowing into the sea.

Yes, you can pray without words and "be" without words. If anything, words interfere with communication at this level, like static in a radio signal.

Having once discovered this for yourself or having been taught this and having sought it, you discover that it is possible to be in a state of constant, mindful, and totally wordless prayer.

Try to empty yourself of yourself and turn it all inside out, until there is no "us" and no "them", anymore, until there are no words.

Pray your prayers straight into the heart of the Living God and receive back the knowing and the peace that passes all understanding.

This is where miracles occur and time and space cease.

This is where you discover the hidden power of The Kingdom of Heaven.

Here is your native ground, your truth, your natural way of awareness and connection– all without words, in a realm of absolute and instantaneous truth.

There are no lies without words. There is nothing hidden.

Last night for me and at noon in Rome, the Great Palatine Seal, which has kept men in chains for centuries and which was meant to keep men in chains for centuries more, was ruptured to the core.

Some of you have learned to pray without words, or this could not have happened so soon.

Keep praying without words, keep emptying yourselves, keep inviting the True and Living God to fill your minds and hearts with wisdom, courage, and love.

Ask for the guidance you need and ask for the coming of The Kingdom of Heaven to the Earth.

Do it without words. Visualize everything at first and then let go of even the visualization — until there is only the pure sense of health and love and all good things abounding.

Answers to Common Questions and Misconceptions for the Jural Assemblies

1. Misconception Number One: that colored people and women are not welcome to join State Jural Assemblies.

This idea derives from the fact that to be on safe ground legally and lawfully, the State Jural Assemblies need to go back and pick up where at least some of them left off -- in 1860. They need to re-establish a Quorum of Jurors qualified by 1860 standards, and that Quorum then needs to update the membership rules to officially include people of color and women.

Please note that in the days of slavery there were both white and colored slaves in this country, and "indentured servants" too --- none of whom could act as State Electors.

The real qualifier was land ownership and neither slaves nor indentured servants could own land, hence, could not act as Electors.

However, both black men and Native men who were Free and who owned land in a State, could act as State Jural Assembly Members and still can.

The important idea behind all this was that nobody not tied to the State by commitment to the Land of that State should have a voice in the affairs of that State.

If you think about this, it is a reasonable requirement: otherwise, people passing through the State could cast votes with no skin in the game. They could, with a large enough population of transients (known as "residents"), dictate to and obligate those people who are actually committed to living in and building their businesses in that State.

We see some attempt at this with the current Border Crisis, where people foreign to the State and with no actual material commitment to say, California, are influencing public policy and helping themselves to public assistance and dictating elections --- all with no substantial actual and material commitment to California.

This is why our States all require Electors to hold only one citizenship --- State Citizenship. They also require State Citizens to be landowners. Color requirements as such, don't actually exist in the American States and never did, except in limited portions of the Deep South.

The more potent issue in 1860 and today is the capacity in which we are acting.

The affect of having the Territorial Congress arbitrarily "confer" citizenships on people and then claiming that they are acting as "persons" via a process of undisclosed enfranchisement, has established a situation in which average Americans are now almost uniformly "presumed" to be in the condition of either indentured servitude to the Queen, or slaves owned by the Municipal United States Government, or both.

It isn't until we take action to Expatriate from any such presumed federal citizenship that we can actually own land in fact, and therefore qualify as State Citizens and as State Electors.

The question of the landownership requirement continues to be contentious. It has been argued in some States that our bodies are made of "dust" and "to dust returneth", and therefore all men and women are "landowners". This may serve the esoteric point, but doesn't answer the actual dilemma posed by non-landowners voting on issues that don't impact them, but which do impose increased tax burdens on landowners.

Women in Europe and America were able to own land and had been able to own land for centuries prior to 1860, so landownership was not the crux of the matter for women. It was more the prevailing idea that women were gentle and needed at home, ill-suited to the hurly-burly of politics and demands of public office, that kept them from being included in Jural Assemblies.

Now that two World Wars and the Civil War itself have convinced us otherwise, women have claimed (and earned) equal rights, and merely updating the old State Jural Assembly rules suffices.

It's a small burden to find 30 free men above the age of 21 who are claiming their birthright political status and who are land owners, to hold the first quorum meeting for each State Jural Assembly, but it is one that assures that the further actions of the Assemblies going forward are properly sanctioned and brought up to date.

And in no case does any of this prevent anyone at any time from: (1) expatriating from federal citizenship status, (2) participating in the State Jural Assembly organizational activities and meetings, (3) making sure that their Assembly is fully staffed, fully informed, and on firm ground going forward.

2. Misconception Number 2: that people have to give up things like Social Security payments or medical coverage owed to them by Federal Government agencies, if they reclaim their birthright political status.

Most Americans never knowingly left their birthright political status. This was merely a self-interested legal presumption being misapplied to millions of people based on equally self-interested falsification of registration documents and improper demands that we "apply" for Social Security, "register" to vote in what appeared to be public elections, and so on.

Having to take action to rebut this legal presumption is anti-intuitive to most people and
the resulting confusion is paralyzing, especially
when they assume that they will lose pension
dividends and health care and other things of
value that they are owed.

Fortunately, the only thing we lose is the ability to vote in private elections hosted by foreign
corporations, which is quickly made up for, as
we hold our own public elections, instead.

Once we return our Given Names (also known
as Trade Names) to the land and soil jurisdiction of our States of the Union, we are no longer
in La-La-Land, and we can no longer be "presumed" to be in the Queen's service or the
Pope's.

All the franchises they have "gifted" us with
are similarly under new ownership--- American
ownership, not "U.S. Citizen" ownership.

The only impact this has is that both the
Queen and the Pope and all their employees are
now obligated to obey the Constitutions and the
Public Law of this country again, with respect to
you and your assets.

The magic words are: "I accept all gifts and
waive all benefits."

"Benefits" are gifts that come with strings

attached-- unseen, unstipulated, undisclosed contracts and conditions that you are "presumed" to know and accept when you accept "benefits".

Thus, when they mischaracterize Social Security Earned Dividends that you and your employers paid for as "benefits" they are claiming that you are acting in the capacity of a "U.S. Citizen" or "Citizen of the United States" --- and moreover, that you are a Federal Citizen in receipt of welfare.

Now, there are many people receiving "benefits" from the Social Security Administration as public assistance that they never earned. Some never contributed a dime and are receiving thousands of dollars in medical care and support payments every month.

Those of us who unknowingly signed up for Social Security and vested in this program meant for Federal Employees are not in receipt of "benefits". Anything we get back is an "earned dividend". The import difference is that "benefits" can be discontinued at whim, whereas "earned dividends" owed to former employees have to be paid.

The situation is analogous to going to work for a foreign corporation in a foreign country. While you are in that foreign country, you obey its laws. You also obey the internal "laws" of the corporation you work for.

When you quit or retire and return home -- what happens?

You are no longer living under the laws of that foreign country, and are back living under the laws of your own country. That's for starters.

The corporation you worked for still owes you every bit of your pension plan.

That includes medical services (not benefits) and monthly dividend payments (not benefits).

It's the same way with Social Security and Medicare. They still owe you every jot, and they owe it to you as "earned dividends and services", not as "benefits".

Similarly, the franchises and ACCOUNTS held in YOUR NAME and created "for" you have been mischaracterized as belonging to "U.S. Citizens" and/or "Citizens of the United States".

These franchises and ACCOUNTS are toxic to you until you return home to the land and soil of your State of the Union via expatriation from any Federal Citizenship, and claim ownership of them as an American State National or American State Citizen.

It's the difference between "benefits" and "earned dividends" again.

As a "U.S. Citizen" or "Citizen of the United

States" you are obligated to pay all the bills related to these franchises and ACCOUNTS created in YOUR NAME, but as an American State National or an American State Citizen, you are the inheritor of the assets and credits owed to these accounts.

Suffice it to say that as long as you cling to your identity as a "U.S. Citizen" or "Citizen of the United States", you are a Pauper by definition, obligated to function under foreign law, obligated to obey foreign corporation policies, obligated to pay for every whim of the British Territorial Congress--- but when you reclaim your birthright political status, you are owed the return of everything that is rightfully yours.

Your Trustees, the British Monarch and the Pope, have to act as your Trustees again ---and return your "borrowed" property, plus interest, leases, fees, etc.

So, you lose absolutely nothing of any importance when you return to your birthright political status, and you regain all that was stolen and commandeered, including your Constitutional guarantees.

As you will be conducting your own elections and dealing with your own issues and taking control of your own purse strings, you will not need to overly concern yourself with the circus in Washington, DC, and you will have no reason or desire to participate in their political parties.

The world will come back into focus and the tail will stop wagging the dog once enough people understand the circumstance and take the necessary action -- (1) reclaim your birthright political status; (2) join your State Jural Assembly and boot it up.

https://national-assembly.net/

Jural Assembly - How to Get Started
https://www.youtube.com/watch?v=QRZzy3bqLRU

How the States Can Save America
https://www.youtube.com/
watch?time_continue=5&v=td7SXuv1LG8

Funniest Trump Can't Win Complilation
https://www.youtube.com/watch?v=G87UXIH8Lzo

What's Happening to Trump?
https://www.youtube.com/watch?v=LaYzx4Dpv3U

Just Wild: The American Form of Government
https://www.youtube.com/watch?v=GGk6LG0GA4A

Q - We Are The Plan
https://www.youtube.com/watch?v=MRtEgdgj_XQ

The Pilgrims gave us a blueprint for a successful nation. Kirk Cameron in Monumental
https://www.youtube.com/watch?v=kSb1q_4KZII

Q - The Plan To Save The World (old version)
https://www.youtube.com/
watch?time_continue=1&v=6cYZ8dUgPuU

Made in the USA
Las Vegas, NV
12 September 2021